MW00877592

Also by

Jeff M. Sambur

A Wandering Jew Follows St. James
A Wandering Jew Nee-Me-Poo
Push-bikes, Heat Waves, & Bushfires
The Stalkers of the Weminuche

Copyright © 2011 by Jeff M. Sambur
ISBN-13: 978-1466482449
ISBN-10: 1466482443

Destroying Demons on the Diagonal

by

Jeff M. Sambur

DEDICATION

To my mother, Clara, who taught me how to smile. To my father, Sid, who gave me his hummingbird-like energy. To all the cancer survivors I have met throughout the years. You are truly an inspiration to me.

ACKNOWLEDGEMENTS

Thanks to all the wonderful folks who allowed me into their busy lives for a few days. Your generosity, kindness and friendship were appreciated. Plus, it was a bonus not to be eating bar food for a day.

Thanks to my friend, Sara Fryd, who helped me complete this book. See her work at sarafryd.com.

Thanks to Kay Lum for her wonderful map work and cover design. See her work at kaylumdesign.com.

A special big thanks to my awesome editor, Kevin Duggan. He managed to take on this project while balancing the life of newspaper man, husband, father, and dog owner. He made the book so much more readable.

Thanks to all of you for taking the time to read this, too. Who knows? Maybe there will be a Seattle-to-Key West cross-country sequel one day.

CONTENTS

PROLOGUE

The voice shot out of the walls with an extra sense of urgency. "Engine Seven! Westside ambulance! Respond to a report of three children buried in a cave-in."

In a monotone, the dispatcher called out the location and map coordinates as we made our way to the engine. I hopped into my rookie firefighter jump-seat as Marty and Kevin got in the cab. The sirens blared the moment we hit the street.

When we arrived on scene, we found a brushy, sandy hillside on the cusp of a residential subdivision. The youngsters apparently had been imitating miners as they dug horizontally into the slope. Unfortunately for them, they weren't aware of the need to use shoring in a mine. The resulting cave-in buried two out of the three lads.

A few good citizens were in rescue mode when we arrived. One of the kids had been pulled out of the sand hill alive and seemed to be doing well. The second boy was lying inert next to the fortunate one.

I shouted to the Good Samaritans, "Keep digging! I'll bring this boy down and come back to give you a hand." With that, I lifted and dragged the sand-encrusted victim down to the other crew members.

"He's not breathing! Can you start CPR? I'll go back and help get the last one out."

I slogged back up the slippery slope. The citizen rescuers had done a monumental job of scraping and had exposed all but the boy's head and upper torso. I grabbed the child's limp legs and with a bystander's help, popped him out of Mother Earth. I hauled victim number two down and started the rescue breathing of CPR with a paramedic from the westside ambulance.

"Let's load and go!" the lead EMT ordered after a few minutes of negative results. We placed the gray-skinned youth on a backboard and onto the main cot. We all piled into the back of the ambulance and resumed the sad task of performing CPR on a child. The ambulance pitched and rolled down the highway as we administered IVs, oxygen and hope. "Come on, kid! Breathe!"

For days afterward, the sound of my voice and repetitive questions became all too familiar to the nurses in the intensive care unit at Poudre Valley Hospital.

"Is there any change in their status?" That was followed by a wishful, "Any improvements in their condition?"

The sad reply was, "Sorry, Jeff; no change." Neither of the children regained consciousness.

It didn't take long before I hardened to life in emergency services. Post emergency patient-status checks became few and far between.

I found out a few years later the parents of one of the boys had divorced. Shortly after the split up, the former wife and mother took her own life, thus claiming victim number three.

About 28 years after this call, I strode away from Poudre Fire Authority and out of its Station 14 for the last time. It was a crisp, wintry January morning as I entered retirement and a new freedom. I headed west to the foothills of Fort Collins, Colo., to go for a trail run.

The sun had just risen and the hills shined with an amber luster. A hawk flew overhead, screeching into the breeze. I took this as a good sign of my future without emergency services. At mile 4 of my run, a mixture of rain and hail blew in, screwing up that omen. No matter; I was still feeling optimistic and giddy.

It took more than a year of doing grownup things (dealing with health insurance, pension plans, house maintenance) interspersed with a few adventures to arrive at that anticipated moment. I was ready to propel a bicycle across this great land we call America.

My schedule would be loose: Leave sunny San Diego on May 8, 2009, and arrive in Bar Harbor, Maine, before the onslaught of the first snow. I planned on taking major detours to cheer at minor league baseball games and spend time in cafés and bars chatting up my fellow Americans.

I wanted to see some roadside attractions and maybe a few natural wonders and enjoy the solace and peace of mind I receive from the simple act of riding a bicycle on a quiet road. That was my dream during all those years of emergency-service work, and it was going live.

During the course of writing this book, I sent a rough version of the epilogue and first chapter to my nephew, Keith. He is a deep-thinking New York City lawyer who looks at the world in a different light than I do. I knew he would provide me with an honest critique and some helpful suggestions.

A few weeks went by and I received no response. Finally, I had to act. I gave him a call:

"Did you get a chance to read the stuff I sent you? What do you think?"

"U.J. (Uncle Jeff), what is the statement you are trying to convey?"

This was a new one for me: I always felt one needed to be a person of above-average intelligence before one could make a "statement." I would never classify myself in that way.

That being said, if you can find a statement in the following pages; that is well and good. If not, please come along anyway. I hope you will enjoy the ride.

California Dreamin'

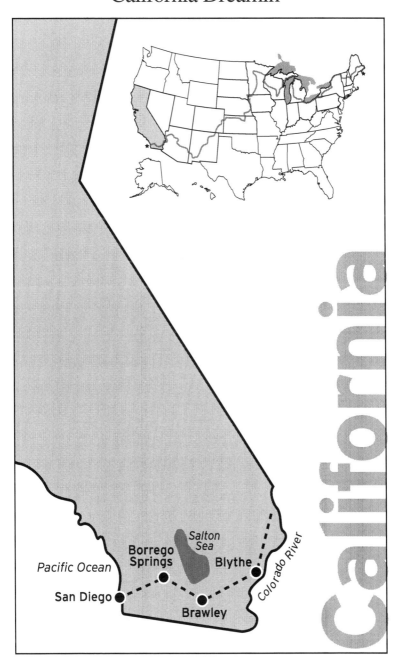

1. California Dreamin'

"Engine Two! Westside ambulance! Respond to a terminally ill cancer patient in respiratory distress. The patient has a 'do not resuscitate' order in her home. A Hospice representative is on scene now. Address is …"

It was an early evening call. The season was spring-ish with a rumor of summer. We rolled out of Station Two following in the wake of the westside ambulance. In a feeble attempt at not disturbing the cancer-ridden woman further, we shut down our sirens and lights a fair distance away.

The paramedics led the way in. We went about our usual tasks: One paramedic spoke to the Hospice saint and I went along with the attending paramedic. We took seats on opposite sides of the stricken woman. She slowly glanced up and made eye contact with me and then the paramedic.

I took her vital signs as the paramedic placed a high-flow oxygen mask over her nose and mouth.

Her skin was the color of an old-fashioned wax candle. She seemed too young for someone about to be robbed of so much. Her breathing was forced and strained, the scene quiet and respectful. The only sound denting the silence was the flow of oxygen moving from bottle to mask.

In a flash of motion her hands shot up to the sides of her face as she did an all-too-real imitation of the painting "The Scream" by Edvard Munch. She let out one, pain-induced gasp and was gone to the great inevitable.

It was a sight I will never forget.

At San Diego International Airport, my old biking buddy Brad was on hand to pick me up. He would be my host and companion for the first few days of my journey.

Brad is an easygoing California dude, despite the chaos of his lifestyle. I watched as he successfully juggled text messages from an ex-wife, four live-at-home kids, work, and a new girlfriend. It wore me out to watch the action.

Brad is also a cancer survivor. It was after the 2001 edition of Ride the Rockies that fair-skinned Brad noticed something was amiss with his lip. He had a sore that wouldn't heal, so he went to a dermatologist for a consultation. The results from the biopsy rocked his world. Brad had desmoplastic melanoma, a rare form of skin cancer.

Brad explained what happened next: "My cancer was 2- to 3-millimeters thick. The surgeons went in and removed half of my lower lip and a corner of my mouth. After surgery, I went through 40 radiation treatments heavily drugged on morphine. The treatments caused my body to consume itself. I went from weighing 202 pounds to 162 in eight weeks. I lost a lot of muscle, too. I could hardly bench press a 40-pound bar, let alone ride a bicycle."

He's what I consider an everyday kind of hero. I'm proud he calls me a friend.

Our plan was to collect two out of four of his children and take in a San Diego Padres baseball game. Is there any better send-off for a cross-country ride?

At Petco Stadium (never did see a dog there, other than a hot dog), we met my senior-citizen friend, George.

I've had the pleasure and honor of knowing George for 20 years. We once pedaled across Iowa on that moving fraternity party called RAGBRAI, or Register's Great Bicycle Ride Across Iowa. During beer stops between cornfields, I listened to George offer words of wisdom from his impressive repertoire of life experiences. It's no cliché; George truly thinks outside the box. He, too, is a cancer survivor.

When I met both of his sons, I had to ask: "What was it like having George as a dad?"

Gary and Rich thought a minute before Rich gave me an answer: "We had to hide our pot really well!" Gary nodded in agreement.

My favorite George line goes like this: "Everyone talks to themselves. It is only a problem if you say, 'What?'"

I hadn't seen George in three years. His hair was whiter and he had a few more age spots adorning his complexion. He ambled along with a pronounced limp. On the plus side, his mind and laugh were as youthful as ever.

We took our seats and played catch-up between pitches.

"I don't like to drive much these days," he confided. "I tire too easily."

"Are you still up for that Wisconsin bike tour in 2011, when you turn 80 years old?"

Riding in America's Dairy Land had been a dream of George's since he turned 75.

"Not sure about Wisconsin; it's kind of hilly," he admitted. "I might be able to pull off that flat Katy Trail ride you told me about."

"Whatever you decide, just say the word and I'll be there," I said.

At the end of another Padres loss, we said so long. I watched George slowly hobble away. I was saddened to discover that even a character like George can grow old.

After a rough night's sleep for me on a too-short couch, Brad and I headed west from his house. We were on a mission to visit the beach and abscond with a vial of genuine Pacific Ocean saltwater.

I planned to carry that sample with me through all the miles and states of my tour. At the Atlantic Ocean, I'd ceremoniously deposit the fluid into that other great body of water.

I know – very cliché: But it would make a grand photo-op. I just wished I had a classier receptacle than a Scope mouthwash bottle.

That chore completed, I spent the rest of the day packing my bike. While performing this act, I looked disdainfully at my camping gear. An idea struck me and I grabbed my maps and laptop.

Hmm … if I did a half-twist here, followed by a dog-leg there, I could make it to settlements with hotels all of the way – no camping required. I felt better already. Where is it written that a bicycle tourist must sleep on a half-inch foam pad on dirt and pebbles? I gleefully shipped my 8 pounds of camping gear back to Fort Collins.

On the appointed day, Brad and I headed east from San Diego in what he described as "May gray" weather. I didn't care; the moment for motion had arrived.

Before long the city traffic decreased and the heat, hills and sunshine increased. Somewhere around Ramona I made my first startling personal discovery of the trip: Avocados grow on trees, not bushes. No wonder I never had any luck cultivating them in Colorado.

We took a banana-and-water break at San Ysabel. At the supermarket, friendly natives spotted my pannier-encased bike and asked, "Where are you headed?" My answer was simple: "Maine! But I won't get there today." I knew I'd get lots of mileage from that line.

We continued climbing to Ranchita, where the heat began to thump us. I noticed a volunteer fire department station that was manned.

"Let's pull in there for some water. Firefighters are always helpful when they can be," I said all too knowingly.

In the shade of the apparatus bay, we met Gary, a polite, friendly and helpful 20-year-old. He was cheerful despite being only half way through a six-days-in-a-row work session. While handing us bottles of water, he told his story.

"I get paid 100 bucks per shift to be here. I'm hoping that all this experience will land me a job with the San Diego fire department. Heck! The other day we extricated the sheriff out of her vehicle after she crashed into a telephone pole. Where else can you get emergency service experience like that?"

We wished the youngster the best of luck in achieving his goals. I didn't tell Gary that I was a firefighter many years before his dad ever had a date with his mom.

From the fire station we inched our way upward to a precipice and then careened 9 miles downhill to Borrego Springs. Waves of heat welled up from the valley floor as if someone had opened the door of an oven baking cookies. The views could have come from Steven Spielberg's cosmic imagination.

The oasis of Borrego Springs was 76 miles into the trip. We secured accommodation at the aptly named Hacienda del Sol, where Brad promptly napped his way to dinnertime. When he came to, I refrained from giving him a hard time about his siesta. After all, anyone who beats cancer is one tough human.

The next morning the sun was soon up and the temperature gauge set on roast. I loaded an extra gallon of water on my rack as an insurance policy against the elements. We moved along quiet roads. The nearby San Ysidro Mountains seemed to leap out of the desert floor. I didn't notice any obvious trails to their summits.

At Ocotillo Wells, we couldn't help but think we were seeing a mirage. There was a speedboat and a snowmobile parked on the desert floor. A sign next to these improbable objects stated, "Dry dock."

A few miles later we stumbled upon a monument noting the Juan Bautista de Anza National Historic Trail. Apparently, we'd been on and off of it since Borrego Springs. The trail commemorates the 1,210-mile journey of 200 settlers comprised of 30 families from Sinaloa, Mexico, to San Francisco in 1775-1776. Once they got to the place that would become the City by the Bay, they founded a mission and a presidio.

At the Los Puertecitos marker we learned Juan and his brave compadres had camped in a nearby wash. As I gazed out at the utter harshness of the land, I considered the depravities people will undergo to get a great deal on real estate.

We rolled on and turned southeast on busy Highway 86. Off in the distance we could make out the Salton Sea.

The history of the Salton Sea is an interesting and disturbing tale. In 1905, the Colorado River breeched a dike in the Imperial Valley. For almost two years the entire flow of the river emptied into what was once known as the below-sea-level Salton Sink. A plug was finally made to stem the flow, but not before a few towns, railroads and plenty of Indian land were submerged.

Now the Salton Sea gets saltier and more polluted by fertilizer running off adjacent farms every year. It doesn't help that the New River flows into this mess. Many believe it's the most polluted stream in the United States.

While pedaling by, I could only think this was surely one heck of a mistake of a salt lake.

At a gas station in Westmoreland, Brad and I chanced upon Larry, an off-duty U.S. Border Patrol officer. He was on a bike of another kind – a Harley – and was making his way home for the weekend.

"I was in the aviation field for many years, but got frustrated with the layoffs," he said. "The BP is a stable job. After all, people are always going to try and get across our border."

Between sips of pop and bites on a burrito, he continued: "It's a pretty neat job. We head into the desert and look for sign: you know, footprints, empty water bottles and discarded clothes. Last night, we caught 20 coming across."

I asked Larry if things had changed much since he's been on the job. He thought for a moment and smiled: "Yeah! Some of them carry cell phones and if they get into a bind, they call us to give themselves up. The other day, I found a dead one in a ditch; guess he didn't have a cell phone."

We moved on and shortly arrived in the Imperial Valley city of Brawley. We were officially below sea level. From this point on, it would be all uphill for me.

The Imperial Valley is an agricultural powerhouse. More than 100 years ago, someone figured out the recipe for growing food and fodder in the desert: It's simple – just add water. The valley's lush green fields would not be possible without the elaborate plumbing system of cement-lined canals, pumps, check dams and pipelines. All of this life-sustaining liquid is supplied by the Colorado River, a resource so sought after it has the dubious distinction of being the most litigated river in the world.

Back in my hometown of Fort Collins, I lived a few hours away from the Colorado's headwaters in Rocky Mountain National Park. I once took a hike to see the birthplace of this Southwest troublemaker. It took a few miles and some effort to reach a narrow creek that even I with my short legs could leap across.

A tiny bridge forded the bare trickle of moisture. Next to the bridge a sign announced, "Colorado River." I am not sure if a

National Park Service hydrologist, jokester or both were responsible for that placard being there.

The mighty Colorado nearly reaches the end of its line in the Imperial Valley. It's a river that hardly ever mingles with the sea.

For Brad, Brawley would be the end of the line for accompanying me. A few hours after we arrived, his lovely girlfriend, Christina, drove east from San Diego to rescue him. From then until who knew when, I'd be going solo again. Brad said he'd check on me throughout my trip.

"Dude! I miss touring," he said. "That was so much better than work!" Amen, brother.

I left Brawley when the sunrise was letting out its first yawn. Once again I loaded my bike with a gallon of water and an array of moisture-laden fruit. Off I set among the acres of alfalfa, wheat and produce. A truck hauling a load of sweet onions blew by. The onions' thin skins flew off the truck like desert snow. I saw a lone farmer pry open a headgate to release precious fluid to nurture his fields. A few minutes later I crossed the East Highline Canal. I was in what Mother Nature intended the Imperial Valley to be – a desert.

Signs along State Route 78 got my attention: "WARNING! Stay on road! Live Bombing Range!"

I looked up at the crystal-blue sky for fly-boys zeroing in on me. None sighted. I felt pretty safe since it would be un-American for the Air Force to bomb someone on Mother's Day.

After the threat from above passed, I entered Algones Dunes Wilderness. On the side of the road an impressive array of snowplows were parked. They were waiting to keep the next sandstorm from reclaiming Route 78.

The dunes undulated and rippled with the Chocolate Mountains serving as a backdrop. It was a scene of incredible loveliness marred only by the clamor of ATVs and dirt bikes.

My feeling of serenity was further shattered when I entered the Glamis general store and met a clerk who was a not-so-jolly fat man. I purchased an overpriced orange juice and asked if I could top-off my water bottles. His answer was short and curt: "No! We don't give water away, we sell it. This is a desert, ya know."

A desert? Really? No wonder there was so much sand, heat and little to zilch vegetation around here.

I left in a semi-huff and pedaled past the Mesquite Mine. From the look of the stout fences and concertina wire, I guessed they were not digging for salt. I discovered later the mine produces more than $100 million in gold a year. No wonder there were no "Free samples" signs.

I was pretty parched when I arrived at a Border Patrol checkpoint. An overzealous German shepherd on a short (thank God) leash lunged at me. A friendlier officer asked if I was a U.S. citizen. He waved me through. It was then my turn to ask questions. "Can you guys spare some water for my bottles? Please?"

"Sure! Would you like ice in them?"

Score! I was finally getting something back for my tax money from Uncle Sam.

While taking sips in the shade of the checkpoint's carport, I made small talk with the officers. I watched their drug/bomb/illegal migrant-sniffing hound in action as motorists came through. The 80-pound nose and its handler sprinted around a vehicle as it pulled in. The dog took a short leap here and a duck down under there in search of contraband. The driver was allowed to continue.

"Does the job ever get boring?" I asked.

"Well, as you can plainly see, we are pretty much on the edge of nothing," an officer said. "The time goes by a lot faster when we have vehicles coming through. We even have bicyclists like you. The other day about 20 came by."

The men were all young, earnest and conveyed a feeling of really wanting to make a difference in the quandary that is America's borders.

From there it was suck-it-up time. Like a spaghetti western movie, I passed Buzzards Peak just in time to have a vulture swoop down to check me out. "I'm not dead yet!" I shouted to the scavenger. He wheeled away looking for a quieter and stiffer meal.

After seven hours of plugging away, I eased into Blythe. From the smile pasted to my sweat-stained mug, one might have thought I found out Jennifer Aniston really preferred me over Brad Pitt, anyway.

The highlight of Blythe was doing an effective job of hiding from the heat. An air-conditioned movie theater featuring the latest "Star Trek" episode helped. Yes, I am a Trekie.

I hit the road prior to sunrise once again to beat the heat. Six miles into my ride, I noticed a plaque on U.S. Highway 95. The sign announced that the first legal claim on Colorado River water occurred here in 1877. Whose name was on the claim? You guessed it; Thomas Blythe.

Mr. Blythe was a wealthy developer/financier from Britain. He had a vision of turning the Colorado River valley into another bountiful Nile River valley. I wondered what old Tom would say if he saw the elaborate plumbing system the Colorado River had become. Think he would be proud to see this once wild river so tamed?

I moseyed on and saw signs of the ubiquitous species known as the Great American Snowbird. Groups of doublewides appeared along the river's edge. Street names such as "Paradise Cove" and "Margaritaville Lane" said it all. Apparently, not all the early-bird special folks felt this way. I noticed one estate's moniker was "Rancho-not-so-much." Below it was a "For sale by owner" sign.

Miles later I turned east across a small graffiti-stained bridge spanning the Colorado River and a borderline. I had arrived in Arizona. So far, so good.

Angling Around Arizona

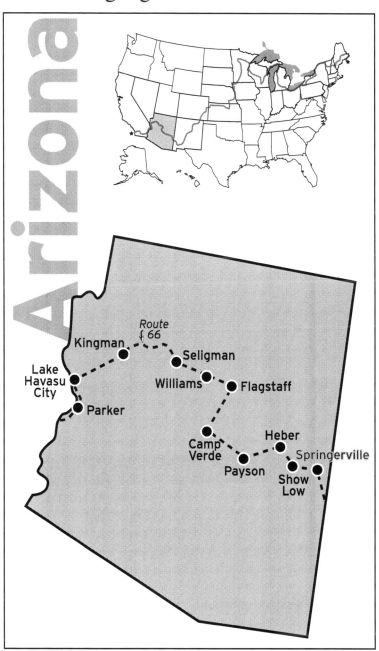

2. Angling Around Arizona

Red lights rudely came on followed by a woman's calm voice: "Engine Four! Respond to a report of a vehicle on fire at …"

Brad, my boss, Elizabeth the driver and I groggily tumbled down the stairs to our awaiting apparatus. Dispatch began to fill in the details.

"Caller told us she saw a car smoking but the precise location might be sketchy …"

I groaned, "Not another Twilight Zone call!"

That was the unlovable nickname I gave to Station Four's response area. In the years I was assigned there, I witnessed more suicides, domestic squabbles, suspicious fires and other Rod Serling-esque calls than anywhere else in Fort Collins. That part of the city seemed to be a repository of weirdness. I should know: At that time I owned a townhome within its boundaries.

We arrived at the address the informant had passed along to dispatch. With sirens still squawking and emergency lights performing a light show, we found no smoking vehicle.

Brad barked a few commands: "Elizabeth! Let's shut down the lights and sirens. We'll do a few laps around the nearby streets to see if the car's around. Jeff! Keep an eye out."

Brad radioed dispatch about our intentions. We glided along a silent street when I spotted something. "Brad! Let's go back around the block."

There it was – a sedan buried in a bush and in the initial stages of fire. We all went from slumber mode to action mode without even stretching.

"Jeff! Grab a hose line!" Brad yelled.

I waved him off: "Not yet! Let me check out the vehicle first!"

Flames flickered below the hood as smoke filled the passenger compartment. I couldn't see crap through the windows. I yanked the driver's door open and through the cloud of smoke I saw someone behind the wheel. He was sitting in restful sleep mode, like I had been minutes before.

I pulled the driver out of harm's way and went back to search the vehicle. "Brad! We have a patient here. Call the medics."

I gave the car a quick search. Once satisfied it was clear, I went back to check on the patient. Brad started putting wet stuff on the small fire.

It was a rude wake-up call for the driver, who was covered with red welts and not much else. With patches of snow on the ground, the season required more than his nudist-colony look.

"Where are all your clothes and how did you get those bruises?" I said.

"I was jogging!" was the ridiculous reply.

"Without sneakers at 3 in the morning? Come on! You can do better than that!"

The police and a medical unit arrived on scene soon after that. We pitched the "jogger" onto the main cot of the ambulance and away we went. The alcohol vapors wafting off "Joe" soon permeated the enclosed space.

After a primary and secondary assessment of him, the only apparent problems were too much drink and too many black-and-blue owies.

Then this strange man became belligerent.

The story unfolded later. "Joe" was literally caught with his pants down in bed with a married woman. The irate husband appeared with a baseball bat to separate the lovers. The home wrecker made a hasty exit and apparently passed out in his getaway car, which made a sudden stop in the bushes and caught fire. Someone noticed this odd phenomenon and dialed three numbers – 911. We all met in the Twilight Zone.

On the follow up, I discovered the man managed to dodge a driving-while-intoxicated charge. Seems this low person knew people in high places.

Maybe I should have stuffed him back into his smoking car.

After crossing the Agnes Wilson Bridge and the state border, I continued riding north through the Colorado River Indian Tribes reservation. The reservation has four distinct tribes: Hopi, Navajo, Mojave, and the Chemehuevi. The residents make their livings from the soil. I was fortunate to be there when the alfalfa was in its purple bloom and the air was perfumed with a heavenly scent.

Of course, these days no reservation seems complete without a casino: The CRIT is no exception with the Bluewater Resort and Casino in Parker. Its vision quest is to separate dollars from tourists, and I am sure it is quite successful. There's a reason why gambling joints can afford to leave their lights on all of the time.

After 54 miles with a tailwind assist, I came to a halt for the night in Parker, an easygoing agricultural/tourism, blue-collar town. A night there didn't ready me for what I'd see on the Parker strip and beyond to Lake Havasu City.

Once again I struck out early to get in a few miles prior to becoming parboiled. I watched as the light of sunrise drew out a palette of colors from the ragged desert mountains. These natural wonders did not last as subdivisions and golf courses became the norm along the river. The Emerald Island green of those 18-hole playgrounds stood out in shocking contrast to the subtle grays and olive greens of the desert's flora.

In Colorado, we go on occasional water restrictions so white-pants-wearing golfers in Arizona have the opportunity to give chase to a small dimpled ball. Oh well; I'll shower once per week to help the cause.

I decided to veer off to see Parker Dam, the manmade obstruction that forms Lake Havasu. It is also the deepest dam in the world. Similar to the proverbial tip of the iceberg, only a small portion of the dam shows. The majority of the earthworks had to be excavated well below the river's base level. We Americans are very resourceful when it comes to constructing dams.

I rode to the top of the dam to shoot some photos of the impeded river. Two security guys wearing polo shirts and driving a golf cart politely asked me to pedal along. Neither of them would have struck fear in the heart of any terrorist. Couldn't Homeland Security afford a macho Humvee for them to cruise around in?

Lake Havasu is the source of water for two major diversions. One split leads to sunny and thirsty Southern California. That project is known as the Colorado River Aqueduct.

The other "straw" is more impressive – the Central Arizona Project. The CAP starts at the Mark Wilmer pumping station and moves many gallons of heavy liquid 824 feet uphill. Place 5 gallons of water on your back and attempt to ascend that distance and you'll soon see the enormity of this engineering marvel. The liquid gold flows to where most Arizonians reside – Phoenix and Tucson. Seeing this up close and personal made me realize the Western adage "water flows toward money" rings so true.

Miles later I plunged toward the shores of Lake Havasu City. It's a modern burg having been founded by Robert McColloch of chainsaw fame in 1964.

Bob must have been some character, similar to P.T. Barnum. He bought London Bridge for $2.5 million and had it reassembled across a canal and the Colorado River. The desert can do strange things to people's minds.

I paid a visit to this out-of-place landmark. I can report that it is not falling down as claimed in the popular nursery rhyme. Visitors strolled by snapping photos while torpedo-sized carps floated near the water's slimy surface. I chatted up a young British couple on their honeymoon.

"Were you folks sipping gin and tonic when some American bloke walked out of London with your bridge?" I asked.

"No, he could have that one. Rumors were he thought he was getting the Tower Bridge. We'd never sell that!"

For a kitschy good time, visit this European icon in the shockingly bright sun of the Southwest. It's no mirage and you won't need a passport to get there.

Lake Havasu City is famous (or infamous) for being a spring break destination for college kids. Think Frankie Avalon and Annette Funicello in the desert, but with a twist. I doubt that '60s crowd did Jell-O shots or shouted, "Show us your ..." to the pure and chaste Ms. Funicello.

At 5:30 a.m. the next day it was already 87 degrees and the sun had not yet risen above the surrounding mountains. I was in motion at that crazy hour for a prolonged day of pedaling. I had a date to keep with a mother, and we all know it's impolite to keep mom waiting.

The matriarch I am referring to is old U.S. Route 66 – the highway immortalized as "The Mother Road" in John Steinbeck's Pulitzer Prize-winning novel "The Grapes of Wrath."

I followed Highway 95 north through desert scenery that would have been appropriate on Mars. I even spotted a mountain shaped like the state of Michigan minus the Upper Peninsula. I turned west on Interstate 40 (I know – the opposite direction of Maine) to the junction of Route 66.

At first, it was only me rolling east on the fabled highway along undulating worn-out pavement. I half expected to see Steinbeck's Joad family bound for the Promised Land of California from Oklahoma. Instead, I saw heaps of motorcyclists and rental cars plowing along the road. Obviously, Route 66 is now a tourist attraction.

I climbed out of the low desert along the Colorado River and into the high Arizona desert. I felt the heat lessen to a bone-chilling 90 degrees. The roadside attractions were few. I rode past a derelict couch inviting folks to "set awhile" and all-too-prevalent memorials to unfortunate drivers who weren't able to negotiate the road's curves. I saw one cross that read, "Ivan. 2001-2005." This can only be the death of innocence.

Hours later, I arrived on the outskirts of Oatman. This relic of a town was named after Olive Oatman, who was captured and enslaved by the Mojave, Apache, or Yavapai tribe. History is open to debate on this issue. However, there's no debating the seasonal boom this former gold-mining town experiences from the resurgence of Route 66.

Outman's buildings are a hodge-podge of shacks, doublewides and a smattering of solid-looking structures. It would not have been a stretch of someone's imagination to view Oatman as an enclave for some end-of-the-world survivalist cult.

On Main Street, tourists and burros mingled freely. It was easy to spot the tourists – they were the ones carrying cameras. The burros were descendants of pack animals miners left behind when the gold played out.

I sidestepped donkey poop as I made my way into the General Store. As I paid for my food, I asked the clerk about the Oatman burros.

"The Bureau of Land Management allows about 1,200 of the burros to roam free between here and Vegas," he said. "When they go higher than that, they round 'em up and put 600 up for adoption. Then the whole process starts over again. The ones that hang around here know I don't like them. They always find my truck and leave a few loads of crap outside my door."

While we talked, a local with a gray ponytail dropped a wad of bills on the counter to pay for a 12-pack of Bud.

"Wife's sick, car dealer repossessed my pickup truck," he said. "I'm going home to get drunk." Many a country/western song has been written along those same lines.

I went outside to see well-intentioned tourists (mostly from overseas) feed the burros carrots, also known as burro grub. These so-called wild burros aren't a bunch of dumb asses after all.

I regained my bike before the High Noon Shoot Out on Main Street began. That was one piece of Americana I could pass up.

It was a climb to 3,500-foot Sitgreaves Pass along a ragged road lined with gold-mine operations. Hours later I rode into Kingman with a sore bum and tired legs. Route 66 could use a new coat of asphalt and a bit of TLC.

Kingman was founded in 1882. It's named after Lewis Kingman, yet another surveyor and railroad man. It's a western town proud of its link to Route 66.

Pretty much every business in town was adorned with the distinct black-and-white 66 sign. Shops, restaurants and motels featured garish paint jobs and vivid neon signs proclaiming their offerings. It harkened back to carefree "Ozzie and Harriet" days. It made me grin.

I decided to work a visit to the Route 66 Museum into my busy schedule. This was time and money well spent because of the museum's informative, entertaining displays about the Mother Road. Stark black-and-white photos of refugees in the Depression and the Dust Bowl eras showed the grimness of their situation.

Only a tiny fraction of those who were part of the mass migration to the Promised Land stayed in California. The majority returned home after a few months of disillusionment and disappointment.

On a cheerier note, some displays gave an idea of what Route 66 became after World War II – an avenue of escape from the mundane. The freedom of the open road beckoned and Americans responded in kind as Main Street became a haven for vacationers. I must have heard that call, too.

Kingman is infamous for a not-so-natural disaster that occurred on July 5, 1973. A railroad car containing propane ignited while workers were off-loading its hazardous cargo. Local firefighters responded and while attempting to put out the blaze got caught in a violent explosion. They were unaware of the dangers of BLEVES, or boiling liquid evaporation vapor explosion. Three firefighters were killed instantly in the ferocious blast and eventually eight others died from burns. A railroad worker also died and about 90 onlookers were injured. The city water department's office has a mural honoring the firefighters and their ultimate act of bravery. I paid my respects before leaving Kingman.

I headed east once again on the Mother Road en route to Seligman. The road gently gained altitude while I moved toward the rising sun. Gnarly desert flora yielded to a blend of piñon pine and juniper. For the first time in days the temperature wasn't scary hot. The views were large and the traffic tiny; I felt relaxed and blissful.

At the halfway point, I took a lunch break at the Frontier Café and Motel in Truxton. I took a seat and immediately noticed that I stood out from the other patrons. When bicycle touring, I become very tan. Sometimes my skin turns the color of mahogany wood. My fellow diners were naturally brown. I had entered the Hualapai Indian Reservation.

While I waited for my meal, two large Native Americans began slowly chanting and drumming on the tables. The sound was melodic and soothing. A sandwich, salad and entertainment for one low price – such a deal!

About 40 miles out of Seligman I crossed paths with Johan, a 66-year-old retired Dutchman riding a recumbent bike on a Route 66 adventure.

"Before I came to America, I didn't think much of Americans. Now I am planning another trip here. Americans are wonderful people. Your government can do better, though." Johan opined.

I didn't argue with his assessment.

He sported a smile, sun-scorched skin and a black Route 66 baseball cap in lieu of a helmet. I asked him how he would cope with the upcoming heat, vast distances and not even a spit's worth of moisture in the Mojave Desert. He sidestepped my question, saying he preferred to take the road one day at a time. We snapped photos, exchanged email addresses and wished each other a safe journey. Like two ships passing in the night, we continued along our ways.

Seligman is all about the Mother Road. Every nook and crease of most businesses is filled with memorabilia. My favorite was the Route 66 Hawaiian shirts. I would have bought one if not for the harsh treatment it would have received being stuffed inside my panniers. I admonished myself for leaving an iron and board off of my packing list.

It was a glorious morning when I departed Seligman. Then I spotted "him."

"You're the guy in the museum movie on Route 66!" I called, and immediately hit the brakes.

With that disrespectful introduction, I met Angel Delgado, aka the Guardian Angel of Route 66. He had the vision and energy to get the remnants of the iconic asphalt corridor preserved. With his humble and mellow demeanor he charmed the politicians into placing Route 66 on the National Register of Historic Places by decree of the National Park Service.

Angel is a spry, wise, 82-years-young dynamo with an infectious grin. He has an understated way of expressing himself that borders on poetic.

I shook his hand and bowed to pay him the respect he deserved. His reaction was a belly laugh and a sincere, "Thank you, sir. It makes me very happy when someone tells me that. It is only 8:30 and you have already made my day."

Since it was so early, Angel proceeded to show me his barber shop. He used to cut hair and give straight-edge shaves before becoming a spokesperson for the road. The shop's walls were crammed with photos of Angel shaking hands with government officials, Hollywood stars and everyday citizens of the world like me.

"I have been interviewed over 400 times. I'll be on 'Good Morning America' again this coming Sunday," he said. There was not even a hint of boastfulness in this statement.

I got a bystander to snap a few pictures of me with Mr. Route 66 for my personal history. I wished him a fond farewell as I struck out on the Mother Road once again.

That evening I searched for Angel on Google and found this quote from him: "This highway is peppered with tears, it's peppered with hopes, and it's peppered with dreams." Wonderful poetry from a former barber; John Steinbeck would have thought so, too.

About 22 miles later in Ash Fork (Flagstone Capital of the World), I was in dire need of a breakfast burrito. I pulled into a mom-and-pop diner. I couldn't help but notice the severely loaded-down mountain bike parked outside with a Burley trailer full of gear attached to it. I walked into the joint expecting to see the Lance Armstrong of bicycle touring.

Instead, I saw a loner at the counter with a pack of Pall Malls next to his pancakes. I reckoned here was a man who wanted to eat in peace, so I slid my bottom into a booth. I indulged in my burrito as the loner went outside for a cigarette break. I watched him closely as he walked around my rig, slowly inhaling on his cancer stick.

He returned to the café and his coffee and asked me, "Is that yours?"

Bill had a grizzled, gray beard and the ubiquitous greasy ponytail sported by many older white gents living in the Southwest. He wore a faded and smudged T-shirt to go along with a pair of threadbare sweatpants. His pores radiated the smell of cigarette smoke. On his head he wore a sweat-stained "Vietnam Vet" hat. Clearly, he was not your typical bicycle tourist.

"A buddy of mine dropped me off in Kingman from Los Angeles. I made it this far in eight days," he said. "I cover about 15 to 30 miles a day."

"Are you taking 66 to Chicago?" I asked.

"Nope! Just going as far as it takes for me to score a job. I heard there is work in Oklahoma." Bill was a modern-day Joad in reverse.

"I've been having problems keeping air in my tires," he said. "Those no-glue patches don't seem to work."

I agreed with Bill that those patches were worthless. I fetched a spare patch kit off of my bike.

"This should work for you," I said and handed him the kit. He took it without saying "thank you." We adjourned outside to our steeds.

"From here to Flagstaff, it is all uphill," he said as he lit up another smoke. "Well, we'll see you down the road!"

I knew the chances of that were about as high as a blizzard in Imperial Valley. Bill's travels weren't one of wonder or wander. Honestly, I'm not sure why he was on that semi-truck load of a bike, but I knew I was glad not to be tagging along on his journey.

I called it a day in Williams, a town named after the mountain man Bill Williams. I was pleased this Bill was not a railroader, tycoon, engineer or surveyor.

Williams sits pretty among the vast ponderosa pine forests of northern Arizona. It is also great guns about tourism. A road forks north to Big Ditch National Park, aka Grand Canyon. If you don't want to drive, a scenic railroad will take you there. Williams was the last hold out on the Mother Road. It wasn't until 1984 that Interstate 40 bypassed the town. Bill the mountain man would have been proud of the town's free spirit.

I enjoyed a relaxed day watching foreign tourists mosey up and down the vestiges of Route 66. They spoke an array of languages that seemed out of place in Arizona's high country. After all, this was not New York City.

The following morning was chilly at 6,766 feet. I had ascended more than 6,000 feet in four days, and was feeling a bit shell-shocked from the change.

After Williams, groovy old Route 66 morphed into I-40. I had no choice but to ride its shoulder as trucks swarmed by. Halfway to Flagstaff I passed a road sign that proclaimed that point to be the 7,335-foot Arizona Divide. I had no clue to what it was dividing, although I had a swell view of the San Francisco Peaks.

After descending about 300 feet I arrived unscathed in Flagstaff. Old buddies Jenny and Rick would host me for a two-night respite from the bike. My legs and sore bum were in dire need of a break.

Flagstaff is a cool college town (Northern Arizona University) of 60,000 people. It sports a funky and attractive Old Town with many eclectic coffee houses, brewpubs and cafes. It's also a bastion of liberal thought in an otherwise "red" politically inclined state.

I could almost imagine myself living there if not for the long winters and bountiful amounts of "white death" – snow. I shoveled enough of that contributing factor to heart attacks while attending college in Syracuse, N.Y., to last me a multitude of lifetimes.

My friend Jenny and I go back to those "Animal House" days in Syracuse. Through the years we managed to keep a thread of communication open, made easier via the Internet. She has been a happy resident of Flagstaff for more than 30 years. When she moved there she went back to the local university to further her education. All that hard school work paid off as she scored a career out of it. She works for the U.S. Geological Survey naming geographic features on Mars – no kidding.

So what does a cross-country bicycle rider do on a rest day? Go for an eight-mile hike in the foothills outside of Flagstaff, of course. Lean Jenny went easy on me with plenty of breaks as we commiserated on what had become of our shrinking nest eggs. I was pleased to be taking a day off from sitting astride an unforgiving bike seat.

After an early-bird-special dinner, we all crashed at a very sedate time. For Rick and Jenny, Monday morning would bring a return to the salt mines, as in work. For me, it would be a return to the business of forward motion. I liked my job more than theirs. After coffee and a hug from Jenny, it was time to view the red-rock country of Sedona.

It was an easy downhill run with gravity on my side. I was OK with the minimum effort I exerted since I had to save my strength in case I had to ride through an "energy vortex."

Sedona has become a mecca of New Age thought and philosophies. Google "Sedona+vortex" and you will get 38,400 hits. Psychic readings and crystals get plenty of action as well. I was determined to ride through one of these phenomena for the energy lift required to get me to New Mexico and beyond. The closer I got to Sedona, the more striking the scenery became. Hell, if I were a vortex, this is where I'd hang out, too. As I dropped down the canyon, I thought I spotted something blocking the road. This had to be a vortex. I put pedal to the metal to enter it.

I blew through the energy field just before it faded into another dimension. The sensation was similar to taking a multi-vitamin and washing it down with a Red Bull. It was a pleasant buzz, but not long lasting.

In Sedona proper I grabbed a bite amid the gaggles of shoppers. I wondered if they even noticed the wonderland surrounding them.

It was time to move on as the heat index was on the rise. I left all the hubbub of this den of Earth mamas and papas behind me to seek quieter places. I managed to escape without purchasing a crystal or a psychic reading. Somehow I would find a way to cope.

I retired for the night 30 miles down the road in Camp Verde, which is named after an Army fort built in 1865. The town seemed quiet enough now that the Indian uprising has been squelched.

The next morning brought something new and completely different to my tour – honest-to-goodness clouds. For the first time since leaving San Diego, I was able to ride sans sunglasses toward Payson.

Ten miles into the climb my cell phone rang: "Good morning! This is John from the Warm Showers List. My wife and I would be happy to have you spend the night with us in Payson. Call us when you arrive for directions."

Score! I had a place to sleep in Payson with normal-sounding folks. The Warm Showers List is not a kinky sex website but a worldwide cooperative of hospitable people. These are folks who don't mind if a total stranger seeking shelter rolls into their homes on a bicycle. For host and visitor, it's a giant leap of faith.

Before I arrived, though, I had heaps of ascending to do. After 10 more miles of climbing, I could swear I saw Mount Everest on the horizon. At the 6,000-foot mark, ponderosa pine became plentiful. I saw and smelled an elk carcass by the side of the road.

Gravity finally took over as I descended into the valley where the towns of Strawberry and Pine took up space. It was time for a break. I was gnawing away at a fried-egg sandwich when an older gentleman dropped by for a chat.

"Welcome to Pine!" he said. "Looks like you've been traveling far."

"How do you know I didn't start three miles back in Strawberry?" I said with a harmless grin.

With that we exchanged thoughts on riding, hiking and retirement. Steve knew the folks I'd be sharing a roof with in Payson. It is a small world in this part of Arizona. He left me in peace with my egg sandwich after a genuine farewell: "Happy trails!"

Afterward, I went to the local museum to digest and learn a bit about the area. The communities of Pine and Strawberry were founded by Mormons in the late 1870s. The pioneers were following the colonization policy set forth by church leaders in Salt Lake City.

By 1877, almost 400 Mormon colonies were in place throughout the arid west. These pious farmers somehow managed to survive in the nooks and crannies formed by the valleys, basins and plateaus that were bountiful in this harsh landscape. Water and the lack of it seemed to be the binding factor of these outback communities. I marveled at their obvious hard work and utter persistence in following their religious beliefs.

I regained my steed and finished the ride to Payson for my date with John and Loraine from the WSL.

"Hi, folks! Thanks for being kind enough to allow me to spend a night in your wonderful home." I said this as I handed over a bottle of red wine, a six-pack of beer and an apple pie. My dear departed Mom taught me never to show up empty handed at someone's residence.

With that intro, one thankful guest and two gracious hosts began to get acquainted. John and Loraine worked as recruiters for the computer chip designers of Silicon Valley. With the onslaught of the recession, there had been more lay-offs than hiring.

"We haven't had a paycheck in eight months," John admitted. Yet somehow they managed to exude an aura of confidence that things would work out.

"However, now I have the time to pursue my love of blacksmithing. I even sold a few pieces. Who knows? Maybe I'll start to make bicycle frames, too." John said while giving me a tour of his immaculate workshop. His optimism and "can-do" attitude were impressive.

Over dinner and drinks the conversation touched on travel, history, politics, geography, cycling, and then nutrition. This was so much better than sleeping in another Motel 6.

After breakfast, I scored a hug from Loraine and a manly handshake from John. Next stop – Heber. All I had to do was climb 2,700 feet to the top of the Mogollon Rim to get there. The rim is a 200-mile-long escarpment and a major geographic and topographic feature of Arizona's diverse landscape. It was named after a long-gone Spanish governor who ruled the area from 1712-1715. Back then English was a second language around here and the United States wasn't even a rumor. However, it proves once again that even that far back in time, politicians had cool things named after them.

This same trend did not continue with the naming of Heber. When I arrived during a rainstorm, I discovered the tallest building in Heber was the local Latter-day Saints ward. The town was named after Heber C. Kimball, a Mormon leader from the 1880s. The local supermarket didn't sell beer or wine. It would prove to be an early night for me.

I woke to battleship-gray skies emitting wet stuff from above. Rain in Arizona? Who would imagine? A Memorial Day low-pressure system was parked over east-central Arizona. For the next few days, I'd be playing tag with cloud bursts and lightning. It was cold, too. I began to miss the desert.

There wasn't much to see on the rolling ride to Show Low besides lonely doublewides, scattered subdivisions and skeletal, blackened snags left behind from the Rodeo-Chediski fire of 2002. That blaze lives in infamy as one of Arizona's worst forest fire. Show Low and Heber, which are practically embedded in ponderosa pine forests, had to be evacuated.

In Show Low I learned the evacuees had returned and brought their family and friends with them. The place was crazy busy. Can't say it was love at first sight, however I did get a rise out of the way Show Low scored its name.

Legend has it that in 1875, Corydon Cooley and Marion Clark both owned vast tracts of land nearby. Apparently this town wasn't big enough for the two of them. With the simple flip of a card (the deuce of clubs), Clark won and Cooley quietly moved on. We can only dream that wars could be decided so peacefully.

That evening I took a stroll down Deuce of Clubs Road and entered the "One-Eyed Jack" sports bar. I got a strange feeling entering the joint when the conversation ceased and all heads turned my way. I took a seat at the end of the bar and ordered a Fat Tire beer. I glanced at the TVs hoping to watch a baseball game. Instead, there was bald and jowly Dr. Phil spouting sage advice. Some sports bar.

A half a beer later, locals Bill and Mark struck up monologues with me. Bill sported the Arizona look of a gray ponytail and scruffy beard. For an extra eye-opening touch, his front teeth were missing. His T-shirt had a single word on the front and back: Probation.

"I used to live in Alaska," he said. "I knew if I stayed up there, I wouldn't get in trouble with the law. Well, I had to take care of family business around here and got arrested." He never elaborated what he was arrested for and I wasn't about to ask.

He spoke about his son: "He's growing medical marijuana in California. Now, that's a racket!" He said all of this with an illegal smile. There's a prodigy a dad can be proud of. It gives new meaning to the words "family values." Bill had a game of eight-ball calling his name, so off he went. In his wake, Mark filled in to entertain me.

"Me, the missus and my kid just moved out here from Columbus, Ohio," he blurted out in a machine-gun burst of words. He took a swig of Bud Light and continued:

"I had to get out of there before my son turned gangster!" It was a stretch of my imagination to think of Middle America and gangster in the same sentence.

"How was I supposed to know I was moving into a Mormon community?" he said. "Me and my Mexican wife kind of stand out around here!"

Ya think? Mark's oversized body was topped by a shaved pate and tattoos slathered around his bulk. When Mark and family moved to nearby Taylor, I'm sure the residents' reaction was, "There goes the neighborhood!"

After another brew and some local news, I stepped out into the night. Yep, this was a lot more entertaining than so-called reality TV.

I woke and decided to gamble (what else does one do in Show Low) with the weather. Looking up, I saw my chances of getting drenched were statistically high. You might call it a sure bet.

In no time and a few miles, I was back in a piñon pine and juniper landscape. Every so often a subdivision rose out of the hills. Signs announcing "For Sale," or "Huge Price Reductions," or "Make an Offer," gave meaning to the recession's wrath. The worst of the lot was "Bank Foreclosure."

It was a gentle uphill to the summit of Cerro-Montoso pass (7,550 feet) on U.S. Highway 60 en route to Springerville. Trees of any kind became the exception instead of the rule, giving way to fields of straw-colored grass. I had entered the Springer volcanic field, the third largest of its kind in the nation. It's an immense geologic field larger than the state of Rhode Island. (Isn't everything larger than Rhode Island?) The main features were dormant (I hoped) volcanic cinder cones and vents.

The big-sky country views were marred only by a distant coal-fired power plant. The rest of the scene was wild and primal. After crossing the Little Colorado River, I arrived in Springerville, a town large enough to support a McDonald's, Subway and Safeway without the hustle and bustle of Show Low. I liked this place immediately.

The town got its name way back in 1875. It was the site of Harry Springer's store. Poor Harry made the mistake of trusting outlaws to pay back what they owed him. In short order his business opportunity went bust. Just to rub salt in his wound, the locals named the community Springerville. Talk about kicking a guy when he is down.

The one strange thing about Springerville was having dinner at Booga Red's Restaurant on Main Street. As always, I headed toward the bar to eat and drink. (Where else can a solo traveler take a meal without standing out like a leper?) I made my way toward the cantina in the back of the restaurant and glanced around. I felt like I had entered the Twilight Zone and wound up in East Los Angeles.

I try not to be judgmental: However, heavily tattooed and do-ragged Hispanics seemed out of place in Springerville. These pretend rural gangsters slammed tequila shots while listening to heavy metal music. Their conversations were not jovial. This had all the ingredients of an explosion waiting for an ignition source. I felt like a lamb in a lion's den. I ate my dinner quickly and retreated to a mellower place.

I left Springerville under cool and breezy conditions en route to another state. Unfortunately, that breeze was smearing me in the face. It had the makings of a long day in the saddle. I ascended out of the volcanic fields and back into the ponderosa pine forests, eventually topping out at 8,550-foot Alpine Divide. This would be one of the highest points of my tour.

"It should be mostly downhill from here," I thought wishfully.

After dropping off the pass into Alpine, I picked up a hot chocolate for warmth and energy. In the space of a few weeks, I had gone from 100 degrees to 50 degrees, from ice water to hot drinks. No wonder my internal thermostat was working overtime.

A few miles later, I was in another state and another time zone. The sign read; "Welcome to New Mexico. Land of Enchantment" I liked that.

No Problemo in New Mexico

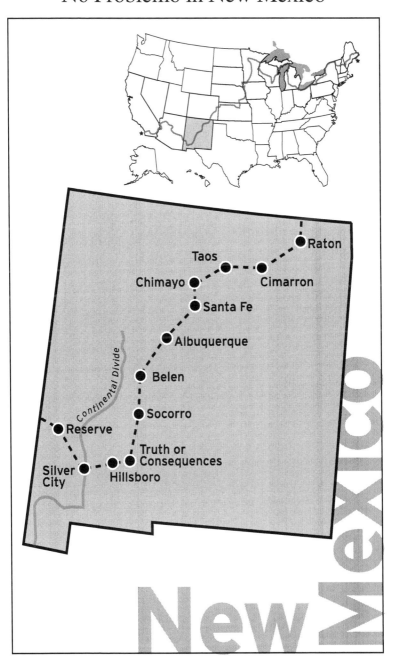

3. No Problemo in New Mexico

"Engine Two, Truck One, Squad One and Battalion One, assist Engine Four en route to a multi-vehicle accident at …"

It was around 3 a.m. March 18 on a crisp, starry and moonless night. A scant three hours earlier, St. Paddy's day had officially ended.

Engine Four had the scene lit up with a combination blue/red warning lights and a bank of harsh halogen lamps providing an eerie glow over what we were dealing with. The hum of Engine Four's generator and the squawking of orders and requests on the radio pack-sets were the only sounds.

Two dogs lay side-by-side next to one crumpled vehicle as if taking a nap in the sun. Camping gear and other personal items were strewn about. The college-age couple sat rigid in the car's front seat, eyes open, staring serenely into nothing. For these victims, there was no luck of the Irish.

The other vehicle had wrapped itself around a large cottonwood tree, apparently landing there after the real damage had already been done. The young man behind the wheel had his eyes closed. He wore a sickening smirk on his face.

There was no blood, no gore and no heroics for us to perform. This was body recovery and a crime scene rolled into one. We stood around feeling sad and helpless as we waited for the coroner to arrive.

An investigation revealed the solo driver had been over-served that St. Paddy's night. His blood-alcohol level was way beyond the seeing-double drunk phase. None of the local watering holes admitted to serving him or seeing him. The unfortunate couple was on the way out of town with his-and-her hounds for a spring break camping trip. I felt sorry for the police-person who had the horrible job of notifying their parents.

A few weeks later I got a call from a fellow firefighter.

"Jeff, remember that call we went on when that drunken scumbag got roughed up by the cops after resisting arrest?"

"Are you talking about the Bozo who was smashing windshields around the university?"

"Yep! That's the same asshole that caused that wreck on St. Paddy's night!"

I hung up the phone and shook my head. That bastard got out of the clink way too soon.

I crossed the Arizona/New Mexico border and the roads immediately deteriorated to potholes and gravel. On the plus side, folks began to give me friendly honks and waves as they sped by.

Being from the neighboring state of Colorado, I had spent many quality days pedaling in northern New Mexico. I enjoyed seeing the mixing of Old West and New Age with a hefty dollop of Spanish influence topping it like a savory salsa. It always felt "right" for me to be in New Mexico.

My first stop in New Mexico was Reserve, which happens to be the county seat of Catron County. This county is one of the largest in the nation (bigger than poor Rhode Island, again) yet one of the least populated. It has more square miles than people.

It didn't take me long to see the sights of Reserve. The one thing no one could miss was Elfego Baca, or at least the bad-ass bronze statue of him. The larger-than-life metalwork shows Elfego emerging from a dubiously small fort with six-shooter blazing, his face set in a make-my-day attitude that would have made Clint Eastwood envious.

The story goes that the town of Lower San Francisco Plaza (now Reserve) needed a healthy dose of law and order after a few rowdy Texas cowboys shot up and tortured two Mexican workers. Elfego to the rescue! He deputized himself, shot a few bullies and holed up in a wattle-and-daub hut called a jacal. Miraculously, he managed to stay alive for 33 hours before the shooting ceased. The bad guys got the message and peace was restored. These acts of bravery came from a 19-year-old who could distinguish the difference between right and wrong.

Later that night, I discovered a Memorial Day weekend rodeo was in town. I went to dinner at one of the few restaurants in town; a barbecue joint. Outside were pickup trucks with "Eat New Mexico Beef" license plates. Inside, big hats and buckles highlighted the cowboys and cowgirls. I noticed no one had ordered chicken or a veggie burger. It was a family-oriented crowd and surely not the type young Elfego had to mess with.

After dinner, I moseyed over to Uncle Bill's for a few dessert beers. I bellied up to the bar as the bartender, who was smoking in front of two "No Smoking" signs, headed my way.

"What's your religion?" he asked.

I was expecting him to ask what kind of beer I drank.

"Jewish!" I stammered, not sure where this was leading.

With that he launched into a few Catholic and Mormon jokes. I guess he spared me from listening to any obnoxious Jewish jokes. I finally got my beer after lamely laughing a few times. I had to pay for that brew with more than money.

The next day brought a great-to-be-alive morning. Gliding past Elfego's statue, I tipped my helmet in respect as I dodged cowboys limbering up for their rodeo events.

The ride was a gentle upward trend toward 6,436-foot Saliz Pass. Nothing to fret over: I was hemmed in on my left by the Mogollon Mountains (that Spanish governor, once again) and on my right by a bank of designer clouds. I couldn't lose either way I looked.

I arrived in Glenwood, which would be my home for two nights. It was time to give the steed a rest. After checking into an expensive dive motel (the Lariat), I took a seat outside and watched Glenwood go by. It was time well spent as Kathy, an impish woman who happened to be cute as a button, stopped by for a chat. We made a date to hike the famous Catwalk Trail the next day. After this friendly and pleasant mother of four left for her campground, I ambled over to the Blue Front bar for a meal and libations.

There I met Mike, a wilderness ranger for the nearby Gila National Forest. He was manhandling shots of tequila and rinsing his palate with Bud Lights. He was a wealth of wilderness and historical data who, unfortunately, had slid into that state of drinking called monologue. I made a few half-hearted attempts at dialogue, but he was too far gone. I sat back nursing my brew and just listened.

"All those folks from Santa Fe and Albuquerque have no clue to what's out here. Yet, they make decisions affecting us locals. Used to be a man could walk into a bar and drink, play pool and smoke. Now we can't smoke …" He continued on and on.

He then groused about the difference between wilderness and green space, the misquotations of conservationist and author Aldo Leopold and a few other tangents. When my head was full, I walked by him, gave him a friendly tap on his shoulder and said, "I think Edward Abbey was your hero."

"How did you know? Sure liked reading old Ed's stuff," he said.

I woke early to move to a cheaper yet nicer motel. After dropping off my bike, I walked downhill to the Golden Girls Café for breakfast. The sign in front proclaimed that it was the "best breakfast in town." It served the only breakfast in town!

I sat down and said a friendly "Good morning!" to the only golden girl in the café. She mumbled a "Good morning!" back while wiping off a nearby table. I looked over the menu and ordered a breakfast burrito.

"Do you want beef with that?"

I was still in Catron County, where "Beef! It's what's for breakfast" is on the menu.

"No thanks! Eggs, potatoes and green chili would be great."

"No beef?" she said accusingly.

"I'd rather not have any beef, please."

A few minutes later, a ground up steer emerged wrapped in a tortilla. There were no eggs or potatoes, just lots of bull. OK! A splash of salsa served as vegetables on top of the mess.

I have been bicycle touring for more than two decades. I've been at it long enough to know that without calories there is cessation of forward motion. I'd never allow that to happen. I ate the tortilla-encased bovine and had a clean plate to show for my efforts.

Kathy showed up and gave me a morning hug and off we went to hike the Catwalk, a designated National Recreation Trail. The route got its unusual name for the water pipes that once snaked through narrow Whitewater Canyon. The water supplied hydropower for the once-booming mining operations nearby, and the pipes needed constant maintenance. The poor fellows who performed the task would balance on the "catwalk" line of water pipes. Now a suspended walkway leads into this scenic canyon.

We left most of our fellow day hikers behind when we turned into the south fork of Whitewater Creek. It was lovely place and a great change of pace from riding. Enjoying a creek-side picnic with easygoing Kathy was pretty special, too. It seemed so long since I spoke to someone for so many hours. After hiking out, she dropped me off at my hotel with a hug and a "let's stay in touch!"

I left Glenwood with a vow to one day return to hike and bike around these fascinating mountains. When that time comes, I'll make sure to get eggs in my breakfast burrito.

An up-and-down ride past dry washes and canyons brought me toward the Continental Divide and Silver City. En route I crossed the mighty (not really) Gila River. It's another Southwest stream that hardly ever makes it to its historical connection with the Colorado River. Phoenix and irrigation diversions grab the bulk of its water. I felt fortunate to see it running free and easy before its demise in Arizona.

It was a mellow grade toward the parting of the waters, aka the Continental Divide, near Silver City at 6,230 feet. Compared to the oftentimes above-tree-line scenery I've come to expect in Colorado, this stretch of the divide was anything but awe inspiring. I was too far south and low in elevation for piñon pine and juniper to be on hand. Dwarf and gangly desert bushes occupied the terrain. I took a photo of the sign and pushed off into the Atlantic watershed.

Shortly afterward I was in Silver City, founded in 1870. It doesn't take an Einstein to understand the origins of the name. Prospectors discovered shiny gray silver ore below the steep hillsides, touching off the violent birth of the town. There were many skirmishes between Apache Indians, miners, lawmen and outlaws. Billy the Kid was known around these parts, at the time going by his real name – William Bonney.

Silver City boasts art galleries and Western New Mexico University. Unfortunately, downtown sported many shuttered stores and restaurants. Young Turks strode around Main Street bearing sleeping bags and attitudes. There was an edgy and hopeless feel to the place. Even the brewpub ceased operations prior to dinner.

Needless to say, I called it an early night and sought refuge in my tiny room at the grandiose-sounding Palace Hotel. Next morning, I needed to fortify myself with a huge breakfast for the upcoming tough ride, so I stepped into the aptly named Silver Café. I was the sole patron in the quaint diner: I took this as a negative sign as to the state of the local economy.

As I ingested a real breakfast burrito, I realized the only time I heard English spoken was when the kind waitress took my order. The rest of the time, I was serenaded by the melodic sound of Spanish. Moments like that make me love New Mexico.

I rode into the sunrise and uphill out of Silver City. A few years ago, I drove this route and thought, "This would be a bitch on a bicycle." I was right.

I climbed, climbed and climbed only to lose that precious elevation gain in a brake-squealing descent. My objective for the day was the 8,228-foot Emory Pass. How many times did I have to earn it?

At least the scenery was engaging. After turning off Highway 152, I encountered the Hanover and Chino open pit copper mines. A meager amount of activity was being waged in those colossal maws, a sign of our nation's economic situation.

After hitting this high vantage point, I dropped like the proverbial stone into the valley of the Rio Mimbres. I've seen toilets put out more water than this so-called river.

From this low point the upward trend continued for an eternity only longer to the top of Emory Pass, which is named after another surveyor. The rain and cold made it all so special, too.

Yes, I'll admit it: This pass kicked my ass.

I quickly exchanged my wet and sweaty outfit for a dry one. And then down I went on a wild, curvy and steep drop. At 6,000 feet I began to reheat.

I was on a mission. I had to get to Hillsboro before 3 p.m. or go to bed hungry. (I phoned ahead and they told me as much.) I passed up a visit to the ghost town of Kingston, regarded by many as worth a look-see. The desire for sustenance took precedence over sightseeing at this point.

I arrived with a scant 20 minutes to spare at the Hillsboro General Store and Café, the sole provider of meals in this former mining town of 200 residents. I sat down with an eat-poop grin and ordered two meals: The waitress didn't even flinch as she took my large order. After scribbling my requests on a pad, she flipped the "OPEN" sign to "CLOSED." The village was officially shuttered after another day of business.

Happily, my B&B had extended hours of operation. After cleaning up at the Enchanted Villa, I ambled along tree-lined Main Street. The only sign of human habitation was a few other tourists sitting in front of the barber shop. Otherwise, the streets were empty. As the sun began to set behind the Black Mountains, the local denizens emerged from their adobe homes.

I said a few "Good evenings!" and got back a reply or two. I received the message loud and clear that these folks really didn't want to engage in speech. There is a reason people choose to live in places like Hillsboro – peace and quiet. I got the hint and retreated back to my B&B for some silent rest and relaxation.

After a great night's sleep and a hefty breakfast, it was back to "work" for me. Buzzards were waiting for me at the edge of town in a dead cottonwood: So much for cheery "goodbyes" from Hillsboro. After a few inconvenient hills, I dropped toward the Rio Grande River Valley.

I crossed under Interstate 25 and turned north on Highway 181 only to discover that I've been on the Geronimo National Scenic Trail since the Mimbres River. There was no mention in the brochures on how that wily Apache warrior dealt with Emory Pass.

I headed toward Truth or Consequences passing pickup trucks hauling fishing boats, jet skis and one party-on-a-pontoon cruiser. They were heading to Elephant Butte Reservoir, which contains the backed-up waters of the Rio Grande River.

Many years ago I biked past Spring Creek Pass in Colorado and the headwaters of the Rio Grande. At the Continental Divide surrounded by the majestic San Juan Mountains, its waters run cold and clear, a far cry from what I saw at this low-slung, barely moving manmade lake. The Rio Grande plods on to form the U.S./Mexico border, getting more and more contaminated and toxic as it courses to the Gulf of Mexico.

I rode adjacent to I-25 seeing a wide assortment of hovels with derelict major appliances and vehicles parked in disarray outside. Had the ghost of Geronimo raided here recently?

A short 33-mile ride brought me to Truth or Consequences, a small city that decided to reinvent itself in 1950. It happened when radio personality Ralph Edwards promised to do a show in the first town to change its name to match his popular radio program. Thus,

Hot Springs, N.M., became Truth or Consequences and won the dubious honor. This spa town still has a fiesta each year commemorating the event that placed it on America's radar screen. There's even a city park named after dear old Ralph. Now T&C is famous for soothing hot springs, art galleries and as a roosting area for snowbirds.

I got a room at the Pelican Spa close to restaurants, museums and bars. The room was painted in Peter Max colors of vivid purples, oranges and gentler blues. I wondered if the local Home Depot had a sale on their hard-to-sell colors.

I got another early start for a long haul on I-25 to Socorro. In the late 1500s, this route had a different name – El Camino Real, The Royal Road. For a few centuries this was the rough highway from Mexico City to Santa Fe. Spaniards traveled this way 22 years before the Mayflower landed at Plymouth Rock. It's now honored as a National Historic Trail.

The high desert views interspersed with isolated mountain ranges grabbed my attention. Did those long-ago travelers enjoy these natural wonders, or was it all a drudgery, like a long-distance drive?

A few miles south of Socorro, I wound up perched above the Bosque Del Apache National Wildlife Reserve. I could see that its fields were lush green in the riparian zone of the Rio Grande. The crops being raised weren't for human consumption; they're for the birds! Visit the Bosque between late November and the latter part of February to spy upon thousands of sandhill cranes and snow geese.

I did just that one month after I retired. I woke pre-sunrise and hustled over to the Bosque. It was frigid as a flock of bird-watchers and I stood by an icy slough. In the hazy pre-dawn light, I could make out hundreds of white lumps paddling about the pond. Occasionally the silence was broken by a nasally honk. The sun rose, and by a secret signal only the geese could detect, the whole lot of them went airborne. The sky was blotted white with the mass of flapping wings. I tried to shoot photos of the gaggle while I giggled and chased them at the same time. That scene of freedom in flight will be etched in my mind's eye till the day I depart this planet.

On a more somber note, off to the east of the Bosque is the site of the world's first atomic bomb blast, code name Trinity. A few weeks after the test blast, the cities of Hiroshima and Nagasaki in Japan were nuked and World War II finally came to a close.

Back to a jollier note, I saw a sign pointing to Smokey Bear Historical Park. The once-living symbol of the U.S. Forest Service's fire prevention campaign is buried there. In 1950, the singed cub was rescued from a forest fire in nearby Lincoln National Forest, and the rest is Hollywood.

After 73 miles I secured a cheap motel for the night in Socorro and wandered downtown. Socorro was once a stop-over along the old Camino. The name translates to "help" or "aid." Back in those days, the local Piro Indians were kind and generous enough to give food and water to the migrating Spaniards. I walked around some more until I came to the Socorro Springs Brewpub. This was a kind town after all.

I climbed up onto the world's tallest barstool and ordered a wheat beer and dinner. Between sips and bites I spoke to Robert, a doctor of some kind of science who performed research at the nearby Very

Large Array. The VLA is a radio astronomy observatory. In other words, they are looking and listening into deep space. I had to ask the obvious.

"Are we alone or not?"

The fast-talking Canadian thought for a nanosecond and blurted out, "As of now we haven't heard from any little green men. But then again, we are not really looking for them, either."

What's the point if we can't make a movie out of it, I thought. He noticed my disappointment and said, "However, we think we found the beginning of the universe."

"You mean, the Big Bang?" I said, brightening up a bit.

"Yep!"And then he launched into scientific funny talk and left me in the ozone again.

The next morning, I chose quiet and quaint roads to Albuquerque instead of I-25. In this way, I'd be closer to the original Camino Real route, too. Bonus!

I passed the villages of Lemitar, Polvadera, Vequita and Bosque. The business signs were in Spanish and sometimes – perhaps as an afterthought – in English. Farming and ranching seemed to be the staples of the local economy. The preferred building material was red adobe. By exiting I-25 I had taken a step back in time. The only thing missing was a caravan of settlers on horseback or foot coming up the road.

After 55 miles of bliss, I called it a day in Belen, which is on the Camino Real. Belen is a major railroad hub; about 110 trains per day pass this way on their appointed rounds to the coasts.

While eating a veggie Subway sandwich, I spoke to a motorcycle mama and papa. Actually, the papa didn't want to have much to do with me. They were headed to distant Maine, too. Their timeline was three weeks total from New Mexico to Maine – roundtrip. Mine was three more months one way. I thought my schedule was better.

I checked into the only motel in town and phoned Kathy in Albuquerque. She and a friend were willing to drive south to join me for dinner. Kathy and Laurie showed up at the Becker Street Pub for Happy Hour. Before I picked up a round of brews, Kathy gave me a massive full-body hug. It was a fine start to Happy Hour.

It didn't take long before the friendly Belenese were handing us advice on where to eat, drink and dance. One pony-tailed dude gave us some insider information: "Come back on Thursday night for buck-a-beer night. This place is packed!"

We adjourned to Pete's Mexican Restaurant, where we ate, told stories and generally enjoyed ourselves until we noticed we were the only patrons left. It was 8 p.m. on a Saturday. I suppose if one is looking for nightlife in Belen, better be there on a Thursday evening.

My companions dropped me off at the Super 8 with a promise that we would meet again. I was beginning to think Kathy liked me. My table manners must have been adequate.

On Sunday morning, I took the back roads into Albuquerque and passed through the Isleta Indian Reservation and past its casino. Miles later I knew I was getting closer to "Duke City" by the number of junkyards, auto-repair shops and other eyesore enterprises usually found on the outskirts of cities that popped up along the road.

I continued on Highway 47 until it morphed into Broadway. I noticed "gated communities" along the way, as in metal gates on the doors and bars on the windows; not the signs of a genteel neighborhood. Ironically, the parking lots of churches were overflowing. As I got closer to downtown, the property values appeared to increase along with the Yuppie factor.

I hooked east on Central Avenue and ran into my old friend, Route 66. The Mother Road skirted by the University of New Mexico and the usual Bohemian-type shops, bars, coffee houses, and pizza joints associated with college kids. Further east, the detritus of the route could be seen with garish neon signs advertising motels and diners.

I kept going so I wouldn't be late to meet an old boss from the fire department, Kirk, who was my first captain. His love of the job rubbed off on me in that early stage of the game. It was an attitude I kept for almost 20 years before the fire service lost its new-car smell. Like so many other careers, it became work. I hadn't seen Kirk since he retired in 1994.

Almost 72 years old, Kirk still sported a trim marathon-runners build. He still got out and jogged 70 miles each week. His tan face had a few more high-desert creases and his hair was a tad grayer, but other than that, he hadn't changed much.

Over coffee we caught up on each other's lives. I filled him in on the deaths, retirements, promotions, divorces, and rumors of our former comrades at Poudre Fire Authority. We spoke about our future dreams.

At dinnertime, we headed over to Kathy's casita for a rare home-cooked meal. For me, seeing the vivacious Kathy again was like a second helping of dessert. It was a lovely way to spend an evening.

I left Albuquerque after saying so long to my stoic former boss and one-time mentor.

"Be safe! Keep in touch!" he precisely ordered.

"Will do, captain!" and with a quick handshake I aimed north to Santa Fe.

The ride was a nondescript, mostly uphill haul on busy I-25. I arrived worn out and salt-stained at the adobe home of Jeff and Tracy in New Mexico's capital city for a two-night stay. I didn't mind the fact that hard-working Jeff managed seven restaurants and two brewpubs. Good eats and drinks were coming my way.

I met Jeff and his sister 22 years ago when they were bicycle touring in New England. I was riding solo when I pedaled into them. We joined forces and rode together from Portland, Maine, to Boston. We managed to keep in touch through years of work for the both of us plus a wife and kids for him.

After I cleaned up, we gathered his family and headed to downtown Santa Fe. Jeff, who is a generous man, took me and his clan to his showcase restaurant, the Rio Chama. Over calamari, scallops, key-lime pie and fresh ales (just like my typical dinner, only different), Jeff told me about his clientele.

"The New Mexico State Capitol is close by. Gov. Bill Richardson and other politicians come here regularly to hobnob. We even have a private room for the governor and his guests. When the state senators and representatives are in session, there's lots of wheeling and dealing in that room. They like their tequila, too."

If the walls of that room could speak they might tell tales reminiscent of Watergate, although in New Mexico style. After all, Lew Wallace, the territorial governor from 1878 to 1881, once said: "All calculation based on experiences elsewhere, fail in New Mexico." The land might be enchanted, but the politics, not so much.

On my rest day I shadowed Jeff while he went about his business of being a successful manager. That didn't last long. I get weary when I watch other people be productive. Being a nice guy, he dropped me off at the main plaza, which happens to be the terminus of the old Santa Fe Trail.

For awhile I dodged tourists, local artisans, transients and pony-tailed Native Americans while strolling among adobe buildings and narrow streets. When a large, ominous cloud loomed overhead, I sought shelter in the recently opened New Mexico State Historical Museum. I soon learned New Mexico's history was a departure from the histories of eastern states.

New Mexico had its indigenous people, of course, was well as Spanish invaders arriving from the south in search of the legendary "Seven Cities of Cibola" and gold. Following on their heels were settlers searching for arable land along the Rio Grande River. Catholic priests chased their flocks into these new lands, too. Converting the natives to Christianity was a goal as well, sometimes by diplomacy, other times by force.

Eventually, the Indians revolted against the new guys on the block. The Spaniards had no choice but to skedaddle back to Mexico.

After many years of fuming, the Spanish reclaimed their colony only to lose it once again when Mexico gained independence from Spain. That arrangement didn't last long as the land was ceded to the up-and-coming United States and its policy of "Manifest Destiny."

New Mexico, which became a state in 1912, also had to deal with warring Apaches, Geronimo and Pancho Villa. Whew!

The museum gave me a chance to get reacquainted with Juan Bautista de Anza, leader of the Mexico-to-San Francisco trailblazing effort. He was the Spanish governor of New Mexico from 1778 to 1788.

After all that newly acquired knowledge, Jeff collected me to attend a family function. His 6-year-old daughter, Ellie, was due to graduate from kindergarten. We arrived at the school in time to see the tykes waiting in the hallway wearing maroon gowns with matching mortarboards. What else would one expect in a state capital that proclaims itself "A City Different?"

The graduates marched into the assembly to the strains of "Pomp and Circumstance" while cameras and video recorders captured the solemn moment. Songs were sung and speeches were given. There wasn't a dry eye in the audience. Good thing Jeff took all of us out to his Blue Corn Brewpub for some rehydration afterward.

In the morning I realized all great things must come to an end, including free beer, food and company. Besides, I had itchy feet. It was time to move along. I parted ways with Jeff after he confided to me, "You have no idea how much I miss those simple days of bike touring." I promised I'd ride for the two of us, and off I went to Chimayo and its famous church.

I had additional incentive to get to Chimayo: Kathy would be meeting me there. OK – you could say I was a tad nervous about this. The ride up Highway 285 was crowded and noisy with traffic. I lost count of the many Indian casinos I passed along the way. Who would have guessed all these Native Americans would have gone from riding the range to becoming croupiers?

Once I turned off onto Highway 503, peace and quiet prevailed. I was on the "High Road to Taos." This was certainly no speedway for cars or bicycles. The landscape was rough and eroded yet easy to admire. I dropped off into a narrow valley where the village of Chimayo resides and found the Rancho Manzana B&B.

There I met Judy, the innkeeper. She was a no-nonsense former resident of Los Angeles with a gentle side. I asked her questions about Chimayo and rumors of drug dealing and gang-related violence.

"It was bad a few years ago, but the community got together and asked the feds for help. They came in with a 'wolf pack' of agents and made 30 arrests. It's been quiet ever since. Unfortunately, Chimayo can't seem to shake that reputation."

I asked her about the *descansos* (roadside memorial) up the road from her place. I noticed that under the dude's name and photo it read "senselessly murdered."

"He was murdered in a drug-related incident. I don't know if you would call it senseless, if you catch my drift. He was murdered elsewhere and his body was dropped there," she said matter-of-factly.

These stories gave new meaning to the term "High Road to Taos." I moved the conversation away from former drug lords.

"How old is that ditch that runs through your property?" I couldn't help but notice the steady trickle nourishing her garden and lawn.

"The *Acequia de Ortegas* (community ditch) was established in the mid-1700s around the same time that the *Plaza del Cerro* (Plaza on the Hill) was built."

In Chimayo the roots really do run deep and old. I thanked her for the local history lesson and headed back to my cabin before my guest arrived.

Kathy showed up and before you know it, two consenting adults were demonstrating affection for one another. At this junction I'll evoke a Forrest Gump quote: "That's all I am gonna say about that."

Afterward, it was time to go to church! On the way over to *El Santuario de Chimayo*, Kathy said, "I'm glad we got that over with. Now I'm not nervous anymore." Truer words were never spoken.

We entered the historic church, which is visited by about 300,000 pilgrims a year. A scattering of believers sat in pews and whispered prayers. We quietly walked around admiring the iconic relics in the main chapel. In an adjacent closet-sized room was a pile of the famous holy dirt, which many believe has curative powers. We saw three generations of a family reverently scooping up the holy substance into plastic bags.

Next door was a larger room where rows of crutches neatly hung from the walls. This was silent testimony to the ill and infirm who were cured by pilgrimages here. We left the sanctuary glad that we, too, made the effort to see it.

In the morning, Kathy left for a business meeting in Santa Fe and I got back to the business of taking the High Road to Taos. I must have been a gentleman as Kathy promised to see me again in Taos.

From the moment I left Chimayo I spun away in "granny" gear to Truchas. It took nine miles and 1,300 feet of climbing to arrive at this village perched on a ridge.

I stopped at the local post office to mail a letter. When I entered, the postmaster was speaking to a customer in Spanish. When it was my turn for service, he switched easily to slightly accented English. I am happy to report that in these small mountain towns the locals have not given up on their traditional ways.

In the late 1980s, Robert Redford's production of the "Milagro Beanfield War" was shot in and around Truchas. I heard that many locals weren't disappointed when the glitz left town after two summers of filming. Yep, it sure would get annoying and boring to see Redford, Ruben Blades and Sonya Braga on a daily basis. I made it a point to leave town before I became a nuisance.

At Penasco, I pulled over to the side of the road to yield for a religious procession. In the lead was a determined-looking woman bearing a wooded cross. Right behind her was a younger woman carrying a plaque with the image of the Madonna on it. These two were trailed by a single-file line of about 50 women of various ages and descriptions. The one apparent unifying factor other than their gender was their unwavering religious convictions. I guessed that they were on their way to Chimayo and its santuario.

I continued on the High Road, which traversed a part of Kit Carson National Forest, before finally descending into Taos. I came in on fumes; the ride was a lot tougher than I thought it would be.

I phoned Kathy and we arranged to meet at Subway for sandwiches. She told me about her business meeting in Santa Fe and I waxed on about my ride on the High Road. We were a temporary couple: It was a comfortable feeling for me.

We checked into a hotel a short stroll from the Main Plaza. After cleaning up, it was time for Happy Hour. We headed to the Taos Inn, supposedly the place to see and be seen in Taos. We made a grand entrance walking hand-in-hand. Over cocktails and small talk, we watched Taos' beautiful people come and go.

From the inn we made out the twangs of electric guitars oozing out of the plaza. We went to investigate and found a middle-aged garage band providing the entertainment as a family-oriented audience roared its approval. We watched as two little girls dressed in pink, Sunday-best dresses performed like mini go-go dancers. There was nothing but smiling faces in that multi-generational crowd.

The band took a final bow promptly at 8 p.m. and we made our way to Eske's Brewpub. Our review: Great food, average beer and a cool Bohemian atmosphere. One has to love a joint where the cook sports cherry-red Raggedy Ann hair.

In the morning, Kathy and I parted ways after a few lingering hugs. We said our goodbyes and once again I was single.

The ride up Taos Canyon to 9,101-foot Palo Flechado Pass was 18 miles. At the base of the climb, a sign informed me that the final battle of the Spaniards re-conquest of their New Mexican territory occurred nearby in 1698. The Taos Indians and other tribes would revolt no more.

Palo Flechado Pass would be the highest point of my journey. At the summit another sign claimed Indians returning from buffalo hunts would shoot arrows into the nearby trees if they scored a kill. I looked around and saw no arrows in the trees. But then again, I didn't see any buffaloes, either.

I dropped off the pass into a park-like valley occupied by the town of Eagle's Nest and a reservoir. The wind hurled me through the scenery. A distance away, I noticed a cyclist approaching, fighting the gale. I crossed the road to meet him.

Scott wore tight-knotted dreadlocks instead of a helmet. Gear was scattered helter-skelter on his bike rack. A jacket fluttered behind him in the wind. The bike's front brake was disabled and the rear tire was bare bones. He carried one lonely water bottle.

"Youngster, you are going the wrong way," I shouted over the wind. "You're taking a beating in this wind. Look what the breeze did to your hair!"

"I know! How much farther is it to the pass? I rode 100 miles yesterday from that "W" town in Colorado."

"You mean Walsenburg?"

"Yeah! That might be it."

"Where are you heading eventually?

"Don't know."

"Son, you need some direction, a new brake and a rear tire, too."

He gave me an innocent deer-like look and no answer.

"Scott, be careful. I don't want to read about you in the newspaper. You seem to be a good kid."

"Thanks for caring. I'll be careful."

We split, him going into a headwind with an unsure destination, me rolling along with a tailwind toward Maine.

In no time I was coasting down the Cimarron River canyon. The river is an underwhelming waterway even by Southwest standards, but the canyon it carved makes up for it. The cliff palisades made a lovely backdrop for a fly fisherman casting gracefully over the water.

I arrived in the town of Cimarron (Spanish for wild or unruly) and the mountain branch of the Santa Fe Trail. For the next few days I'd follow the trail north and east and almost into Kansas.

The Santa Fe Trail was the 1821 brainchild of Missouri trader and merchant William Becknell. He loaded a mule train with manufactured goods and headed toward the plaza of Santa Fe. History fails to mention if he ate a breakfast burrito or drank a microbrew there.

He returned to America with furs and other booty. The trail soon became an international trade route. In 1846, it served as a military road for the bloodless invasion of New Mexico in the Mexican-American War.

Cimarron also was the epicenter for the Colfax County War, a series of battles fought over the breakup of the nearly 2 million-acre Maxwell Land Grant. (Yes, that's larger than poor Rhode Island.) The war involved squatters, shootouts, broken promises, foreign companies, a railroad, the U.S. Supreme Court and one pioneer, explorer and trapper named Lucien B. Maxwell. It was indeed the wild, wild West.

Cimarron is a whole lot more peaceful now. There's not even a bar in which to get into a tussle.

I woke refreshed and stepped outside my room only to meet a rodeo clown, J. Mark Wilson. He calls his profession "bullfighting." His job is to intervene between a raging bull and the insignificant, if irritating, cowboy on its back. J. Mark happens to be a devout Christian as well.

"It's a calling," he said. "I believe Jesus wants me to save those bull riders."

He was a lean, wiry, 6-foot-something wrangler who moseyed with a slight limp. He sported a shock of gray hair – not surprising for someone who gets chased by berserk bovines on a routine basis – and a Tennessee good-ol'-boy grin pasted on his face. What else would you expect from a rodeo clown?

We spoke at length, marveling at what he did for a living and what I once did for a living. We shook hands at parting.

"You are one brave man. I had to go into a burning building every now and then, but I would never mess with a pissed-off bull," I said.

He gave me a final "aww shucks" look and a shrug before I headed east once again.

I followed the Santa Fe Trail, which has the modern title of U.S. Highway 64, with a cooperating tailwind. I was exiting the mountains and entering the plains. Pronghorn antelope appeared near the roadside to act as a welcoming committee. If I could ride like they can run, I'd be in Maine in a few weeks. These "speed goats" have been clocked at velocities between 45 and 60 mph. But they do have "white man's disease." They can't jump.

Almost halfway to Raton, I pedaled into the town of Colfax. Saying it's a town might be a misnomer. There was only one structure left standing – a bar.

I met Rudy shining his Harley-Davidson in front of the tavern. Behind him was a sign announcing, "Colfax Bar Prairie Glof (no typo, that's how it was spelled.) Every Body Welcomed." Rudy was waiting for other putters to show up for the 10 a.m. tee off. I asked him about the big tournament.

"Well, see those barrels out there in the fields?" he said. "All you have to do is hit them with the ball. There are no holes. Last year 40 folks showed up."

I looked over the barren scene and realized the whole course was "in the rough." Rudy didn't say if Tiger planned to attend.

An old friend nicknamed "the Angel" (real name Dennis) Baca set me up with a hotel room in Raton, his hometown. He felt bad that he would not be there to show me around.

This Angel earned his wings many years ago while I was touring in southeast Colorado. On a waterless, foodless and practically scenery-less 122-mile stretch between Springfield and Trinidad, Dennis drove north from Raton to cache sustenance along my route. He even came by and picked off my panniers and dropped them off in Trinidad.

If that wasn't enough, he accompanied me the last 40 miles into town on his metal steed. Now in Raton, he scored me a free room for the night. He might be a saint, too.

I took a walk to Main Street (Second Avenue) where I paid a few dollars for entry into the local museum. Being an inquisitive fellow, I asked the volunteer curator about the Maxwell land grant. He thought for a moment and launched into his opinions and facts.

"In 1992, Ted Turner bought a half million acres of the grant that starts outside of town near the golf course. He moved all the cattle off and brought in buffalo. He stopped the mining operations."

He seemed uncomfortable talking about Ted. I had to ask, "Is Ted considered a good neighbor to Raton?"

"Well, he donated $100,000 to the city…" he trailed off and then walked away. The interview was over.

With my investigative reporting career suddenly terminated, I pulled up a stool in the White House bar and ordered a Bud. Rudy the golfer showed up. I asked him how the tournament went.

"My son and I were doing well, but after a while everyone lost track of the scores. We had a lot of fun though."

We went on to converse about travel, family and friends.

After he downed a shot of Jagermeister, he opined, "Most people are pretty good. The world's not as ugly as most Americans think."

He proved his point by buying me another Bud before riding off on his Harley.

The next morning, insane tailwinds propelled me up and over 7,834-foot Raton Pass on I-25. I was still on the Santa Fe Trail. I spun by a bright yellow road sign that announced, "You are leaving New Mexico. Hasta la Vista!"

A moment later, I stopped to photograph a large brown sign that stated, "Welcome to Colorado." I was back, albeit temporarily, in my home state.

Easing Through Eastern Colorado

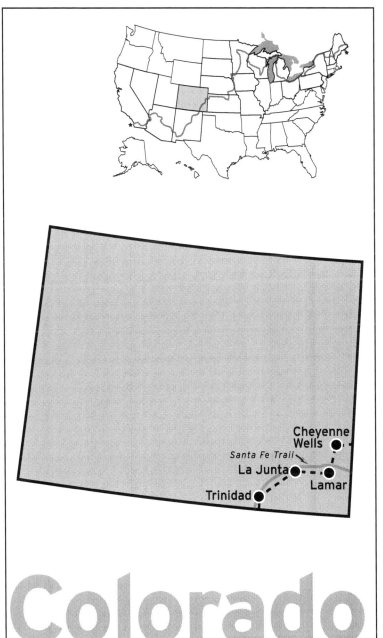

4. Easing Through Eastern Colorado

The alarm came in at wipe-the-sleep-from-your-eyes time. Dispatch was having trouble describing the nature of the emergency.

"Engine Two! Westside ambulance! Respond to a report of four women feeling funny. The address is …"

My boss, Lenny, spoke for all of us when he said, "I feel funny a lot, but I don't call 911 over it."

From the jump-seat our rookie firefighter, Rick, said, "Here, here!"

We arrived on scene with the paramedics and found four women, or should I say two couples (not that there is anything wrong with that.) It didn't take an episode of ER to see the cause of this funny stuff.

On the coffee table wedged among a few candles was a half-consumed tray of hash-laced brownies. We waited while the paramedics performed the Q&A period of a medical exam.

"Does anything hurt?"

"Do you have chest pains?"

The answers were negative.

As we rolled our eyes, one of the patients picked up a phone and placed a call. The voice of dispatch crackled over Lenny's radio: "Engine Two, are you on scene?"

Lenny shrugged and said, "Yes! We have been on scene for five minutes."

"We just received a call from that address requesting assistance."

We chuckled: Apparently we weren't good enough for this emergency. These lesbians wanted the "A" Team for marijuana mitigation. The westside ambulance crew released us from the call. "Not sure what you can do here. Go back to bed."

We did just that.

Over a coffee in the morning, I poured through my emergency medicine manual. Nope! Not one sentence concerning what to do with four stoned-out gay women.

Gravity did its wonders after topping out over Raton Pass. It didn't take long before I was strolling around Trinidad, Colo.

It felt strange to be back in Colorado, a place I called home for more than three decades. Up north in Fort Collins, I had already sold my Old Town home and would be moving to warmer climes in the coming winter. I looked at Colorado with a growing sense of nostalgia.

Trinidad is a historic city sitting astride the Santa Fe Trail that once was the center of a now defunct coal-producing area. There had been some inroads into natural gas production, but with the economic slide, that tapered off, too. On the plus side, as the Las Animas County seat, it is still the hub of commerce in this sparsely populated corner of the state.

It had been seven years since I walked the cobblestones of Main Street. I felt regret at seeing so many shuttered storefronts in that once vibrant downtown. One half of a city block had been ravaged by fire. The buildings' charred skeletons were all that remained. This wasn't a city planner's idea of urban renewal.

One positive change was that the town had a brewpub, aptly named Trinidad Brewing Co. Angel Baca planned to grace me with his presence there for dinner and cold beers. I planned to pick up the tab in appreciation for him securing me a free room in Raton. It's not every day a person can say, "I dined and drank beer with an Angel."

Practical matters came first; I had to secure a roof over my head for the night. A brochure at the Visitor Center caught my eye, or should I say, wallet. "Downtowner Hotel! $32.00/night. Clean rooms, Cable TV."

I rolled over there. In retrospect, I should have seen the warning signs; the tyke bikes, barbeque grills, a weight-lifting bench parked outside the rooms, and a pickup truck with its engine sitting forlornly next to it on blocks. The residents greeted me with "fresh meat" looks. I should have fled but, alas, I allowed my diminishing 401(k) pension make the hard decision.

Dennis arrived and we escaped to the brewpub. While quaffing flavorful Kolsch beers, he told me about his 50th birthday celebration in Denver and his mom's health problems. Real angels worry about their moms.

We struck up a conversation with the Amazonian bartender. The wise guy in me had to ask, "Do people in Trinidad go postal eventually with these crazy winds?"

"Nope! That would require caring. People in Trinidad are too apathetic to notice or care." She wasn't originally from around here. Being new to the area, she came complete with a few new opinions.

After dinner, the Angel flew back home over Raton Pass. I decided to wander around downtown to avoid going back to my dingy room. Of course, I landed in a bar.

At this point I should mention that Trinidad is known as the "Sex Change Capital of the World." It all began in 1969, when a surgeon named Dr. Stanley Biber performed his first procedure making a he into a she. In the doctor's prime, he did four operations a day. I figured that a satirical name for a tavern in small and otherwise conservative Trinidad would have been "The Clip Joint." I ended up settling for Delmonico's.

I was watching the NBA playoffs when "she" caught my eye. Her muscle tone was a bit pronounced, her Adam's apple somewhat severe and she was knocking back shots of Jack like tonic water. The piece de resistance was her voice, almost Clint Eastwood gruff. I finished off my Bud and left. Some mysteries are better left unsolved. Besides, I didn't want the Kinks to write "Lola II" on my account.

The next morning was chilly and overcast and I was bushed and cranky. A family disturbance had spilled out into the parking lot at 3 a.m. There was a lot of swearing, slamming of doors and a car squealing its tires while fleeing the scene. Peace was restored by 4:30 a.m., but by then I was three-cups-of-java alert. Oh well, I needed to get an early start for the 81-mile flight to La Junta along the Santa Fe Trail. But first, I needed black coffee and a breakfast-burrito fix to prepare for tackling the high plains of eastern Colorado. The C&H café came highly recommended by the locals, so in I went.

I'll admit I wasn't in the best of moods when I took a seat at the counter. That began to change when I met Manuel, the 78-year-old owner, waiter, cashier, busboy, and greeter all rolled into one. He was cajoling with Santos, who was 84 years old and in fine form as well. The conversation was animated and energetic. I asked them about their anti-aging secret.

Santos spoke first: "It's the water!" He gushed a belly-laugh as he said this.

Manuel's answer was more serious: "You have to stay busy."

After breakfast, Manuel offered more words of wisdom. He was concerned about me and my bicycle.

"Do you need money? I can help out if you are poor."

"No, no, Manuel. I'm not destitute. I like riding my bike. I'm not a transient, I'm a traveler."

With that he evoked a classic line: "Jeff, you have a great smile. When I saw you, I could tell you are a good man. Remember, life is not about the destination, but the journey."

That's a lot of smarts from a gentleman who flips pancakes for a living. I shook Manuel's hand, took his photo and thought, "Now this is the way to start a day."

I felt fortified on food, caffeine and a dollop of kindness. I was ready to head into the "Great America Desert." That's what surveyor Stephen Long dubbed the vast area east of the Rockies on his map in 1823. For me, this nickname soon rang true as I passed the ghost towns of Model, Tyrone, Thatcher, Delhi, and Timpas.

Along the way were caved-in homes and businesses that hadn't made a buck in some time. I wondered if these were former dry-land farming communities that bought into the whimsical notion that "rain follows the plow." The idea was that humanity could alter weather patterns simply by planting seeds into the earth. It didn't work; hence there are many ghost towns in eastern Colorado and beyond.

I was worn out after six-plus hours of pedaling to La Junta. However, I had a treat to look forward to. Douger, a Fort Collins buddy of mine, had won a free night's stay at the Holiday Inn and gave it to me. I would be staying there for zilch! There were warm chocolate cookies awaiting me at check-in, the wireless connection worked, the room was immaculate, scented soaps and shampoos were there to cleanse my grimy body. An all-you-can-eat hot breakfast would provide me with plenty of calories in the morning. A cross-country bicyclist could get used to this life.

It was a struggle to leave Hotel Paradise, but the Santa Fe Trail called me out of my secure nest. A little east of town, I made a stopover at the National Park Service's replica of Old Bent's Fort on the banks of the Arkansas River.

Here was a prime example of early American capitalism at work. The Bent brothers (Charles and William) and Ceran St. Vrain privately funded the building of this fort to facilitate their fur-trading operation. The wily entrepreneurs exchanged manufactured goods with trappers and Indians for their furs. These transactions seemed to appeal to both parties. Isn't that how capitalism is supposed to work?

Things ran smoothly for 16 years until Charles Bent accepted the appointment as the first American governor of the newly acquired

New Mexico territory. The locals didn't think much of this English-speaking politician and assassinated him in 1847. That was the start of the Taos Revolt. There are a few historical references that suggest Charles might have flunked "sensitivity training" with his strong and biased opinions of New Mexicans and Indians.

Back at the fort, business slowed down. Remaining brother William offered to sell the fort to the U.S. Army. The Army apparently thought the selling price too inflated and refused to pay it, so William destroyed the fort. Talk about a real estate deal gone bad.

The adobe fort is a close facsimile to the original one, complete with folks walking around in period dress. I resisted the urge to take a stack of furs with me on my journey east. A few bananas from La Junta would have to suffice.

While pedaling past Las Animas, I ran into another young man on a bicycle. Trey had both a goal and the Lord, unlike dreadlocked Scott in New Mexico.

"I'm on my way to Grand Lake, Colorado, to meet some friends. I began eight days ago from San Antonio, Texas. I just graduated college and wanted to see our country on a bicycle."

I started to give this earnest young man the lowdown on La Junta, as in the restaurants, hotels and bars.

He replied, "Oh, no sir! I don't drink. I'll usually stay with folks from the local church."

I laughed and said, "That wouldn't work for me. I'm Jewish and there are not a lot of synagogues in this neck of the plains."

He might have whispered a silent prayer for me then. I gave him a friendly pat on the shoulder, took his photo and wished him a sincere God's speed.

After that, a steady westerly breeze aided my transit to Lamar. A glance at my maps confirmed what I already had suspected. I was exiting the Spanish sphere of influence and entering the realm of English-speaking white folks. I was concerned my journey would become more "Wonder Bread" and less spicy salsa.

Lamar is a railroad and agricultural center. It is also the self-proclaimed "Heart of America on the Santa Fe Trail." I spent a relaxed night there. What wasn't relaxed was the bowl of multiple-alarm spicy hot green chili I ate for dinner. It might not have been full-on Montezuma's Revenge I experienced, but darn close. As if I wasn't feeling crummy enough, low-lying clouds, screaming rain, and wind and chilly temperatures assaulted my spirit as well. I was not thrilled about a 78-mile ride to Cheyenne Wells.

I left Lamar and entered the world of wheat that rules much of southeast Colorado. Traffic was light, which meant I didn't have to pay much attention to steering. This allowed me to concentrate on how tired, damp and crappy I felt. Oh joy!

Later, a crop-duster plane strafed me with a dose of pesticides. I tasted and smelled the noxious vapor knowing it could not be good for me. However, there is always a silver lining: Vermin would not feast on me that day.

In Sheridan Lake (which was dry) I took a break from the dreary drizzle. I was shocked to see four pannier-laden bicycles outside the sole store/café. Of course, they were college kids.

"We just graduated school in Hutchinson, Kansas. We're heading toward the mountains of Colorado," one of the kids said.

As always, I handed out fatherly advice about bike touring and wished them bon voyage. I was beginning to think that I was the only cycle tourist with an AARP card in his wallet.

I made it into Cheyenne Wells and slumped into a chair while I waited for the hotel-person to arrive. Yep, I was beat. I paid, got my key and relaxed in a depressingly dark room. I chewed a few more antacid tablets, too.

Many hours later, I was revived enough to venture "downtown" to the Gap Bar. I met Danny, who had just chugged a "Jaeger-bomb." We made introductions and away he went.

"Dude! You're from Fort Collins? That town has great weed!"

I took a slow sip of my Bud and disappointed him by saying, "I wouldn't know." After I realized what I had said, I added, "Don't worry. I am not a cop."

"Whew! Glad to hear that ..." Then he told me about the three years he spent in prison. His crime? A multi-state high-speed chase.

"I was 18 years old at the time. They wanted to put me away for 32 years! Well, maybe I shouldn't have had that 16-year-old kid in my car ..."

Sometimes you meet some interesting people in bars who came from behind bars, even in Cheyenne Wells. That night I got plenty of rest. I would need it for my planned assault on the state of Kansas' highest peak – Mount Sunflower.

It was still gray and clammy when I lit out east on Highway 40. I passed Arapahoe, where there wasn't much more than a service

97

station, grain elevator and a post office. A few miles farther east, I entered Kansas.

"Toto, we're not in Colorado anymore!"

Kan This be Kansas?

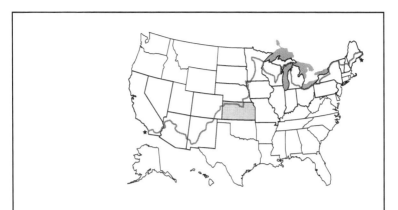

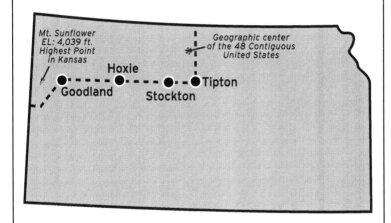

Mt. Sunflower
EL: 4,039 ft.
Highest Point
in Kansas

Geographic center
of the 48 Contiguous
United States

Hoxie

Goodland

Stockton

Tipton

Kansas

5. Kan This be Kansas?

It was late afternoon when we were called out. "Engine-Four! Westside ambulance! Respond to a report of a man trying to hang himself. The informant was very agitated and our info is sketchy. The address is …"

By the time we arrived, dispatch relayed to us that the suicidal man was in the garage. Elizabeth grabbed the med kit while Brad and I went to the garage's side door. It was locked. Brad applied his boot to the door a few times and we gained entry.

Sure enough, a 40-something-year-old man was dangling like a side of beef from an electrical cord. Next to him was his hysterical wife screaming at dispatch via a cell phone. We quickly grabbed his almost limp body and tried to lift him high enough to relieve the pressure between his windpipe and the electrical cord. He wasn't a small man.

Elizabeth hauled over a chair and tried to unravel the cord. We couldn't cut the wire since it might have been "live." We didn't have time to trail the very long cord back to its source and simply unplug it.

With one more heave upward, Elizabeth got the cord untangled from the patient's neck. We began to perform our "ABCs" (airway, breathing, circulation) of EMT medicine. When the paramedics arrived, it was time to load and go.

Elizabeth and I hopped into the ambulance to assist with ventilation, IV set up and the myriad of odd jobs that needed to be done.

That distraught man walked out of the hospital a few weeks later no worse for wear. This was a "save."

His wife threw ice water on our celebrations when she called the chief to complain about the kicked-in garage door. She wanted the fire department to replace it. When our crew was notified of this, we figured there must have been a reason why this poor guy tried to off himself. The reason might have been his wife.

Under threatening white-out condition skies, I decided to go for broke and summit Mount Sunflower. I turned north on to a sandy road. Traffic, people and just about everything stopped. Well, there were heaps of curious cows watching my transit and a whole lot of wheat. The few homesteads were cocooned in nests of cedar trees in half-hearted attempts to block the constant prairie wind.

Six miles of swaying through the dirt brought me to a roadside tombstone. The inscription read, "BOD 1865." Poor BOD must have perished in his/her attempt to attain Mount Sunflower. Obviously, this peak was one not to be trifled with. Carrying that sobering thought, I carried on.

At mile 11, a simple road sign pointed west (toward Colorado): "Mount Sunflower. One Mile." I made the turn and dropped it down into "granny gear" for the final steep ascent. I had to dodge an avalanche or two in that mile and was thankful for my wide tires. I felt a bit light-headed from the extreme altitude. It was just like Jon Krakauer's "Into Thin Air" only different.

From this 4,039-foot-high vantage point, I was able to look down at everyone else in the Sunflower State. I could even make out Colorado, about half mile away. I shot a few commemorative photos and descended to thicker air before hypoxia set in. I had made it!

Three hours later I arrived in Goodland. I haled a man weed-whacking his lawn to ask directions. Thirty minutes went by as Ralph expounded on local history, restaurant suggestions and Goodland gossip. Let the record show that folks residing in Kansas are a friendly mob.

Before I was able to extricate myself from his monologue, I had to ask: "Don't you want to know where I am heading?"

This got his attention long enough for him to ask.

"Where?"

I smirked as I said "Maine!" He halted in mid-speech and thought for a moment "Son! You are in Kansas; people here don't do things like that!"

That evening I headed to Hank's Bar and Grill for dinner. I spoke to Al, Hank's son-in-law (Hank had passed away a few years ago.)

"When the Super Walmart opened they lowered prices and drove the local businesses into the ground," he said. "Goodland and its downtown is now a dying city. The city council is anti-growth and we are stagnating."

Does this woeful tale sound familiar?

After my meal, I walked back to my hotel. I glanced back at Hank's. Sure enough, there was a "For Sale" sign in front. Think ol' Hank would have approved?

I had a very peaceful night's sleep, but that's to be expected after the effort it took to summit Kansas' highest point. I remembered waking briefly while thunder-boomers growled out in tornado alley. When I left for my morning buzz, I then realized the severity of the storms. Ponds had formed in the parking lot, complete with ducks and carp! Worse yet, there was a "Tornado Tracker" vehicle parked next to my room. Somehow, I remained asleep while havoc raged outside.

It was crisp sunny morning as I continued east toward Hoxie. The gods were kind enough to reward me with a westerly blast of wind. The immensity of the Kansas plains was almost hurtful to the eye. There wasn't a lot to break up the vast horizons; only the occasional windmill, tractor, antenna, or grain elevator punctuated the endless flats. I had a feeling I would be missing trees soon enough.

I secured a nice room in Hoxie and called it an early night in the slumbering town. I did wonder what was up with the Confederate flag at Trish's Lounge. Is northwest Kansas that far south?

Next morning, I waded through a drizzle until I arrived at Hill City hungry for a breakfast. I wandered up and down the streets looking for a café but mostly saw "For Sale" signs on the storefronts. Desperation was setting in when I waved down a mini-van and asked: "Excuse me, sir! Are there any places open for breakfast in Hill City?"

He gave it a thought and said, "Cowboy Junction at the golf course on your way out of town."

I thanked him and sped off. Hill City's downtown had surely seen better days.

After Hill City, I was entrenched within the realm of the Solomon Valley/U.S. Highway 24 Heritage alliance. The folks at the alliance claim the river valley is both fertile in history and agriculture. They even came up with a nifty acronym for Solomon: "Stories of Land of Man of Nature." Cool stuff.

A few miles east of Hill City I hit the 100th meridian. That's the longitudinal line on maps that generally separates wet vs. dry, humid vs. semi-arid. As if on cue, unnamed creeks began to bisect Highway 24. In the thirsty west, these precious waterways would have been lovingly named. For the first time in what seemed ages, I broke out in a high-humidity-induced sweat.

Soon afterward, I pulled into Nicodemus, which is named after a hero slave who was able to purchase his way to freedom, and saw a remarkable sight – a real live black person in rural Kansas.

Nicodemus was founded in 1877 by former slaves from Kentucky and Tennessee. They somehow managed to eke out an existence in this harsh land. At the town's high point, it had an estimated 700 people, three general stores, a newspaper, a bank and two hotels. But then the railroad bypassed the town and it withered in the ever-present wind.

About 30 black folks still live full-time in this spot on the Kansas plains. From their valiant efforts to make it happen, Nicodemus is a National Park Service Historic Site.

I arrived in Stockton, where the bait shop kept longer hours than the supermarket. People here can go hungry, but the fish won't. I took my dinner at the Duck Pond Tavern, a funky establishment where the telephone "quacks" when someone calls. How original is that?

I left Stockton in the morning after watching fishermen come and go from the bait shop. Without a doubt it was the busiest place in town. I continued east along the rolling terrain of Highway 24, passing the birthplace of Russell Stover of candy fame in Acton. I exited Highway 24 in Osborne and I felt fortunate to have stumbled upon it for my traverse of the high plains.

From there I turned onto Highway 181 and discovered real, live hills in Kansas, complete with long-distance views. I was on my way toward Tipton for an R&R session on the Palen family farm to spend a few days with Doug, Tracy and their little son, Isaac. I was in need of a break from the steed and a farm stay sounded like a wonderful change of pace.

I met Doug and Tracy when they were on their honeymoon in Fort Benton, Mont. Of course, I was on a solo bike tour. They were having dinner and beers on a restaurant patio when I interrupted their romantic interlude with a few lames offhand comments. I was lucky Kansas farmers are outgoing and friendly at all times. We exchanged email addresses and kept in touch through the years. Apparently, I made a positive impression since as I scored a down-on-the-farm invite.

Before I showed up, I asked Doug politely if it would be all right for me to pass on the milking the bulls chore. I'd heard Kansas farmers have a strange sense of humor.

After I arrived and we got reacquainted, Doug explained that it was "tweener" time on the farm. The fields were not ready to harvest and the seeds had already been sown. He assured me that it was a busy time nevertheless. I was in awe as Doug juggled paperwork, hands-on jobs, family obligations, and phone calls in an effortless manner. He didn't even wear a watch; he measured time with the seasons.

I kept out of his way by helping with a few chores, including a very dangerous chicken roundup. (Just like cattle only on a smaller scale.) It was a relaxed two nights complete with fine dining and Happy Hours when I heard the call of the open road – again.

This would be a special day of riding with not one but two Kansas highlights. I was revved up and excited. My first stopover was back to Highway 24 and Cawker City, aka "Home of the World's Largest Ball of Twine."

It nearly took my breath away when I saw the Volkswagen-sized stringy brown mass. It reminded me of the first time I gazed down into the Grand Canyon, only different. A sign informed the twine-traveler that the ball was started by Frank Stoeber in 1953. It weighs more than 17,000 pounds. Under all these factoids was the motto, "Thrift + Patience = Success." Sensible words to live by from those hard-working Kansans in Cawker City. I was a tad upset when I learned I would miss the "Twine-a-thon," which occurs every year on the third weekend of August. The festival features a citywide picnic, a cook-off and a parade. And, of course, more twine is added to the colossal, frayed mass. One day it will take over the world.

If you plan on going to the Twine-a-thon, I'd advise you book accommodations ASAP for the gala event.

From Cawker City, I detoured northwest to Lebanon. It took 25 miles of riding before the feeling of twine awe subsided a bit. A mile and a half past microscopic Lebanon, I found myself at a monument marking the geographic center of the lower 48 states. Right ahead of me a rusty Pontiac bearing Arkansas plates slid to a stop in front of the historical monument. Soon after, a family of four (sans mom) jumped out and danced around the obelisk. I laughed at the absurd sight.

Phil, the dad explained: "We're doing a Griswold's family vacation. We came all the way up from Wichita to see this."

I had no room to talk since I had pedaled from San Diego to do the same cheesy thing. By the way, the actual geographic center is about half a mile away. Apparently, the farmer who owns the spot isn't too keen on strangers visiting his land.

We snapped commemorative photos of each other and shook hands. I told Phil about the ball of twine in Cawker City.

"Great! That will be our next stop."

I left the monument knowing that I might be at the center of the country, but my journey was far from half over.

A dozen miles later, I glanced up at a sign that stated, "Nebraska, The Good Life." Underneath that was the following information, "Home of Arbor Day."

Good! Maybe there will be more trees to look at.

North to Nebraska

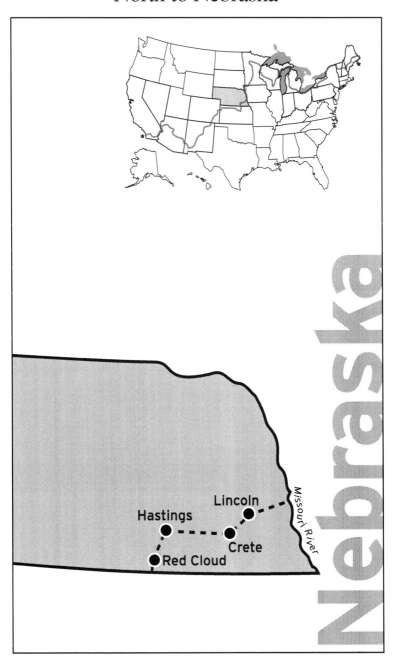

6. North to Nebraska

I was celebrating Thanksgiving at Station Five with turkey and all the trimmings except the beer or wine. Kirk, Steve and I were making a dent in our desserts while watching the traditional Detroit Lions football game.

Sometime during the first quarter the tones went off. "Engine Five! Eastside ambulance! Respond to a report of an unresponsive elderly man. Caller claims the patient appears to be sleeping. Address is …"

We put down our sweets and five minutes later we arrived on scene. As the lead EMT, I had the medical kit and made initial patient contact.

He was an 80-something-year-old senior citizen reclining in a La-Z-Boy lounger. His head was tilted to the side; a splotch of drool stained his shirt. His skin color was somewhere in the vicinity of battleship gray. I glanced back at my crew and gave them a let's-go-to-work look.

We hauled the lifeless form out of his comfy chair, placed him face up on the carpet and began CPR. With the first compression, we heard the unmistakable sound of his brittle ribs breaking – never a joyful noise.

A moment later, the paramedics arrived and intubated the old timer with a hollow breathing tube: IVs lines were inserted and drugs administered. Between compressions, I saw the disbelief and horror in his family's eyes. A few broke down and openly wept; one daughter gnawed at her knuckle. A few attentive mothers shooed their kids from the room.

Fifteen minutes later with negative results, a paramedic called the ER doc and relayed info to him via a phone. He came back and whispered, "OK guys! Let's call it."

The other paramedic placed a white sheet over the departed one. We began to clean up the CPR debris; syringes, bag valve masks, bloody pieces of cotton cloth and used gloves.

We filed past the family one by one saying a lame, "We're sorry. Is there anything we can do?"

The family was too numb to respond. This would surely be a Thanksgiving they would never forget.

Our crew headed back to Station Five and without missing a beat rejoined our desserts. While savoring my pie ala mode, I realized how much the job had hardened me.

Was it my imagination or were there more trees in the Arbor State? The one thing I didn't have to imagine was Webster County and Red Cloud's love affair with the novelist Willa Cather.

Red Cloud is the town where the Pulitzer Prize winner spent her childhood. Now the Willa Cather Foundation resides in a red stone building on Main Street. On the town's outskirts, the Nature Conservancy deeded the Willa Cather Prairie to the foundation in a noble attempt to restore a small piece of Nebraska to its pre-settlers condition. I'm sure Willa would have been pleased.

That evening, Willa fever seized me as I ended up at the Willa Cather B&B Retreat. After cleaning up, I adjourned to the It's All Here Bar and Grill in downtown Red Cloud. While draining beers, I listened to the good-natured ribbing the farmers tossed at one another. It was then that I noticed on top of the bar a mug shot issued by the Webster County Sheriff's Office. I thought it strange the photo was of a smiling black lab dog.

Underneath the picture of public enemy number one was his rap sheet: "Impounded! We will hold for seven days." It went on to state where the culprit was caught and how much it would cost the owner to bail out this bad boy. Obviously, major criminal activity doesn't exist in Red Cloud.

In the morning, I drifted north toward Hastings, largest city I had crossed since distant Santa Fe.

En route, my bottomless pit of a stomach notified me that is was time for a second breakfast. I turned into itsy-bitsy Blue Hill and managed to find Klancy's Kafe on miniscule Main Street. I took a seat at the counter and ordered a slab of pancakes and coffee. The waitress handed me an are-you-kidding-look and hurtfully stated, "Too late for breakfast." It was 9:15 a.m. What time was dinner served in Blue Hill – 2 p.m.?

I returned to the road and met up with a tortoise crossing the road. For my good deed of the day, I moved him to the other side. Only later did I wonder if that really was its intended destination or did I give the little critter a longer commute.

I was later rewarded with the trifecta of U.S. historical trails – the Oregon, California and the Pony Express trails all converging at the same spot.

The Pony Express route was the one that epitomized the spirit of the Wild West. Americans have always been enamored with the imagery of the rugged horseman galloping across the high plains carrying a mail pouch while dodging hostile Indians and dealing with the elements.

Who would not be impressed with the job notification those young bucks responded to: "Wanted! Young, skinny, wiry fellows. Not over 18. Willing to risk death daily. Orphans preferred." In truth, the Pony Express was a blink of time in the American experience. The whole business lasted around 18 months, replaced by that new-fangled invention, the telegraph. I thought about the ride on my metal pony and knew there was nothing express about it.

Once I made it into Hastings, I decided to do a lap around the downtown. There wasn't much there to catch my eye. I learned Hastings was where Kool-Aid was invented by Ed Perkins in 1927. Now the city sponsors a Kool-Aid Days festival on the second weekend of August. While the festival attendees are quaffing Double-Double Cherry and Triple Awesome Grape, they may rest assured they can still reach the Twine-a-thon in Cawker City, Kan., on time.

It doesn't get any better than that.

I left crazy early the next day because I had nothing better to do than bask in the rays of the rising sun. A scant few miles east of

Hastings on U.S. Highway 6, I noticed bread-loaf shaped mounds on the south side of the road.

The earthen, manmade structures are all that remains of the Naval Ammunition Depot from World War II. Back in September 1944, some careless smoker flicked a smoldering butt in the wrong place. The ensuing blast killed nine and wounded 53. The folks from Doniphan (11 miles north) even took notice. See? Smoking really is hazardous to your health.

A peaceful community college and a U.S. Department of Agricultural research center now occupy the site.

At mile 20, I felt the invisible presence of a strong tailwind on my back. I decided to go with the flow. Sixty miles later after passing endless fields of corn, soybeans and alfalfa, I arrived in Crete. No, not the Greek island, but a bucolic Nebraska town of 6,000 souls. After a mellow evening and a good night's rest, I wandered into the 9th Avenue Bar and Grill for my morning meal. It wasn't a beer-and-a-shot type of breakfast but a real eggs-and-potatoes kind. Long-distant cyclists get their sustenance wherever they can. While locking up my precious cargo, I couldn't help but notice the senior citizen breakfast club eyeing me.

I took a table near that gray gang and began to go over my maps. It didn't take long before Jake came by and asked, "My friends are curious about you. Would you care to join us at our table?"

How could I say no to someone's granddad? Little did I know that I'd be joining the Crete branch of the Woodpecker Club for its breakfast meeting. Between the waitress dispensing coffee and taking our orders, I fielded their questions.

One wry-looking gent wearing a mischievous grin and a military baseball cap caught my attention. "Sir? Did you serve in the U.S. Navy?" I asked.

"No son, I'm an admiral in the Nebraska Navy."

"Come on! Nebraska Navy? This is a land-locked state. How clueless do you think I am?"

Of course this drew a round of snickers before Jake intervened: "Meet Gene Harding, former University of Nebraska journalism professor and admiral in good standing in the Nebraska Navy." He went on to explain that the Nebraska governor can grant honorary admiral titles to Nebraska citizens. Gene Harding happened to be one of them.

After exchanging email addresses and taking a few photos, they wished me a sincere "good luck." Those Woodpeckers were kind enough to pick up my breakfast tab, too. It was then that I began to appreciate the birds of Nebraska more and more.

Riding away with a full belly, I met Jay. He was the first touring cyclist I'd seen since Colorado. He was heading cross-country, too; just in the opposite direction. He was an upbeat Californian on a charity ride to benefit the music programs of the Oakland schools. Severe budget cuts had apparently separated the pupils from their musical instruments.

"I can't carry a note, but I love music. It's important for those kids to have a creative outlet," he said.

He wore a camcorder on his helmet capturing his journey as it unfolded. Heck of a lot more high-tech than me. After exchanging information, I said goodbye to this do-gooder. The world is full of worthy causes, isn't it?

I dodged a few drenching storms before arriving in an upscale neighborhood in Lincoln. Pam from the Warm Showers List would be my benefactor for the few days I'd be staying in Nebraska's capital city. Lincoln is also home of the University of Nebraska. GO BIG RED!

Pam had picked up two tickets for the College World Series being played that night in nearby Omaha. Score!

My hostess created a healthy lunch, which we enjoyed at her kitchen table. Even though we had just met, it felt as if we were old friends getting reacquainted after a long absence. Pam was an educated, fit and attractive woman with a gentle smile. Our conversations ebbed and flowed during the 60-mile drive to Omaha.

The College World Series, Omaha, and Rosenblatt Stadium (named after a former Omaha mayor) went together like peanut butter and jelly. Since 1950, it was home of the CWS. Rosenblatt Stadium also had the distinction of being the largest nonprofit ballpark in the country. Unfortunately, this iconic green cathedral was shuttered in 2011, replaced by the corporate-sounding TD Ameritrade Park Omaha.

While in line to use a porta-potty placed near an array of tailgaters, I asked a few young fans how they felt about the change.

"It sucks! So much of the atmosphere of the CWS will be gone. No more tailgaters. No more having brews in neighborhood bars. There probably won't even be on-street parking. All the great things about the CWS will change once the new park opens downtown," they said.

I gazed at the multitudes of happy fans milling around, many of them proudly wearing their school colors. I even saw a Texas Longhorn booster with an impressive set of longhorns on his ample head. I thought to myself, "I'd rather watch a game at Rosenblatt Stadium than a ballpark named after an online stock-trading company. Rosenblatt is a name I can trust."

Pam and I took our seats along the third base line. It was a lovely evening for baseball. We spoke between pitches, did our fair share of people watching, and saw a pitcher's duel of a game. I had spent off-time on the bike in worse ways.

The game's outcome? The Texas Longhorns gored the Arizona State Sun Devils in the bottom of the ninth, 4-3.

Back in Lincoln that Saturday morning, Pam volunteered to show me the sights of the capital city. We took in a Bohemian farmer's market, visited the immense state capitol building, and walked into the home of "Big Red" football. After all this sightseeing, we called a time out to relax and regroup for a night on the town. To sum it up, it was a hoot to play like a college kid again as we hopped from brewpubs to pizzerias to dive bars and finally a martini bar.

Sunday morning was muggy as Pam joined me for part of my ride to Council Bluffs, Iowa. It felt odd to have someone to converse with (other than myself) for 35 miles. I discovered I could still talk and ride a bike at the same time. Between the jabbering and the 15 mph tailwind, the miles breezed by. At a busy highway junction, I thanked and hugged Pam a sincere goodbye. This was one kind and generous woman. The world would be a better place if there were a few more Pams around.

Just southwest of Omaha, I crossed the Platte River before its confluence with the mighty Missouri River. I remembered back to a time 35 years ago when I lived along the banks of the north fork of the South Platte River in Shawnee, Colo. That icy, crisp and clean Rocky Mountain stream did not resemble in any way shape or form the murky soup I witnessed in Nebraska. It had the classic look of "too thin to plow, too thick to drink."

I twisted and turned my way around Omaha's older neighborhoods, new subdivisions and industrial complexes before meeting up with Tod at the Upstream Brewery.

Tod arrived there on a bicycle. He was a friend of Pam's who would host me for a night across the Missouri River in Council Bluffs.

But first we ate and drank. We had our priorities right. Our critique of the Upstream? Fine food and very quaffable brews. With a slight buzz and pleasantly happy stomachs, we crossed the Missouri River on the Bob Kerry Pedestrian Bridge. I straddled the Nebraska/Iowa border and a painted line signifying the states' division.

I gazed down on the swirling, surging brownish-gray current with its Sunday pleasure-boat traffic plying the waters. Could Lewis and Clark fathom what had become of the Missouri River?

I left the Cornhusker State and entered the Hawkeye State.

Inching Around Iowa

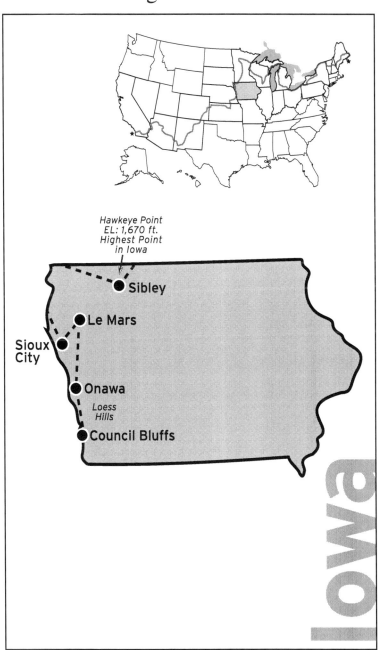

Hawkeye Point
EL: 1,670 ft.
Highest Point
in Iowa

Sibley

Le Mars

Sioux
City

Onawa

Loess
Hills

Council Bluffs

Iowa

7. Inching Around Iowa

"Engine One, Engine Two, truck, squad and battalion chief! Report of smoke in Tony's Tavern at …"

It was a midweek morning when the call came in for this notorious bar. Sure enough, thunderstorm-colored smoke wafted out of the open front door. Our crew donned gear, air packs and masks. We placed a hose line at the door as we filed in to investigate. There was a distinct line of smoke splitting the good air from the bad air at the 4-foot level. I glanced to my left and noticed a table of customers watching us intently. Their heads were well within the noxious fumes. For these professional drinkers, this was an episode of reality TV, only live. Somehow they managed to take sips on their drinks, between gulps of air.

I squatted over to them and intoned through my face mask, "Gentlemen! Please take your drinks and retire outside with them. We'll make sure you don't get in trouble with the police." This seemed to make sense to them, as they grabbed their whiskey glasses, saluted me and moseyed out.

We soon found the source of the smoke – a smoldering pile of rags. We dealt with it and left Tony's.

When we were done, my boss said to me, "Strong work!"

Council Bluffs got its name from an historic meeting between Lewis and Clark and the local Otoe Indian tribe in 1804. No one was on hand to record the exact words that were spoken by Lewis, but in essence it was; "We're from the government and we are here to help you." Yeah, right!

After a no-stress night at Tod's home, I aimed north en route to the Loess Hills Scenic Highway. The Loess Hills (pronounced luss) are an unusual geologic formation. Wind-blown sand from the Missouri River valley and plenty of time formed these hills, which run about 200 miles from Council Bluffs north past Sioux City. To say the 250-foot-tall ridge stands out in Iowa would be an understatement. Heck, there's even a forest worth of trees straddling them.

China's Yellow River valley is the only other place on Earth where this phenomenon occurs. Maybe that's why I craved Chinese food while I made my way over them.

The Iowa weather service had issued a heat advisory for the day, and this was no dry heat. After 45 miles of lovely yet sweaty cycling, I realized I wasn't getting any closer to my final destination of Onawa. Here lies the problem with scenic highways: they don't follow straight lines. I displayed my practical side and took a direct path to Onawa.

In that one-motel town, I dined at the Suds and Jugs Bar and Grill. True to the Midwest's notion of bar decorating, there were many dead animals mounted on the walls. They glared at the patrons with steely, unblinking eyes.

I rolled out of Onawa with the weather service issuing another Hades warning. I poured bottles of water into me as sweat poured out of me. Moisturizer for my flesh would not be an issue.

I followed the Loess Hills Scenic Highway out of Onawa, hypnotized by its serene and green beauty. OK, I'll say it. I was in lust with Loess. I ran the highway more or less north to Moville. Once again, practicality won out as I searched for a more direct route to Le Mars.

In Moville, I sought shelter in a convenience store/gas station when a raging rain chased me inside. A few Moville-ians informed me that, "It'll be a soaker! You'll be getting really wet!" a bit too gleefully.

Why do people revel in other folks' crappier moments? I proved them wrong by waiting out the squall while nibbling on a muffin. After two dozen more miles of undulating fields of corn and soy vegetation, I was in Le Mars, self-proclaimed Ice Cream Capital of the World.

Blue Bunny Ice Cream's world headquarters are in this tidy town. The two largest structures in Le Mars are ice cream related. There's a 5-foot, multi-flavored sundae statue parked outside the ice cream museum and gift shop. For a guy like me, who revels in cheesiness, it made for an obvious photo-op.

As the sun exited for the day, I stopped at the Blue Bunny Ice Cream Parlor, where I purchased a trowel's worth of that wonderful stuff we all crave. The ice cream was so fresh, I had to slap it.

In the midst of all the excitement, I realized I bypassed a ballpark in Sioux City, a personal no-no. I looked over my maps, made a few arrangements, and tweaked my plans to go backward. Sioux City Explorers, here I come.

I was willing to do the bonus miles despite the disparaging comments I'd heard about Sewer City, I mean, Sioux City. This was in reference to the cattle-poop stench emanating from the stockyards.

I arrived with loads of time to spare before the game. I used it to further my education and boarded the dry-docked "Sergeant Floyd" river boat. This former Missouri River conveyance was named in honor of the lone casualty of the Lewis and Clark expedition. Mr. Floyd was buried on a bluff nearby with full military honors.

The ship contains an extensive exhibit on the hazards of river travel on the then-fickle Missouri River. A ripe banana's toss from the museum flow the now placid waters of the Missouri. Any resemblance to the wild river that Lewis and Clark fought on a daily basis is mere coincidence. The U.S. Army Corps of Engineers has given the Missouri a nudge here, a channel there and slowed its flow with many a dam. Those famous explorers would consider it a weak sister to what it once was.

After meandering around downtown, I caught a taxi to Lewis and Clark Stadium. The ballpark is inconveniently set on the southern edge of the city, as if it were an afterthought.

Tracey from the Explorer organization sported me a ticket after I emailed her about my ride. Once inside the very functional ballpark, I realized that finding an empty seat would not be a problem. It didn't take long – the second inning – for the local heroes to get down 10-0. The sparse crowd was more enthusiastic about the hot dog eating contest happening in the stands than the game. I consoled myself by drinking a beer special and getting a photo of me with Slider, the team mascot. The final carnage was 12-4. The Explorers stunk, but honestly the city didn't.

On a Thursday morning, I got another early start to avoid some heat and predicted headwinds. I chose to follow the path of lust, I mean Loess, and continued north along the scenic highway to its demise in Akron.

I was in the midst of a snack-and-water break in a small downtown park when a white-haired man driving a forklift stopped by. "We have ice-cold water at the lumberyard," he said. "Please come by and fill your bottles when you are ready."

That was an offer I could not refuse. I coasted into the obviously named Akron Lumberyard and met Dan the forklift operator and owner.

He cut the power to the forklift and asked me the usual questions concerning the where, when and why of my trip. Then he looked me square in the eyes and flatly asked, "How's it been?"

I was honest when I said that the trip had been beyond my expectations. I went on to expound that we live in a beautiful country occupied by good people.

I explained it this way: "America is not the Fox News reports where you need to be fearful all of the time. For the most part, people have been kind, polite and generous. I have yet to meet anyone out-and-out mean-spirited."

Dan thought about this for a moment and opined, "Yes, good Americans are in that silent majority."

I might not have expressed it with a "Tricky Dick" Nixon paraphrase, but I agreed with the concept. He went on to warn me about some nasty road construction and how I could avoid it. I was glad he didn't hold his tongue on that solid advice.

We shook hands and away I went toward South Dakota to see a flock of melodious yellow birds, aka the Sioux Falls Canaries baseball team.

Short Time in South Dakota

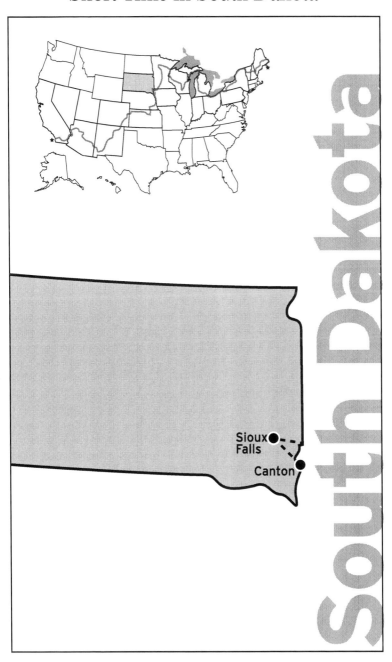

8. Short Time in South Dakota

"Engine Three, Engine Five, truck, squad and chief. Report to a working fire at … We are getting many calls on this."

I was assigned to Engine Five at the time. After dropping a five-inch supply line to Engine Three, firefighter George and I grabbed a backup line and headed inside the roasting house, a newer two-story affair in a better-than-average neighborhood. It wasn't quite a McMansion, but more of a wannabe. Flames were visible from outside the house and putrid smoke billowed out the front door. We dropped to our knees and somehow found the stairs. Our mission was to look for fire extension on the upper floor – pretty much standard operating procedure.

We grunted our way upstairs and heard the hiss of steam as Engine Three's crew applied wet stuff to the red stuff on the ground floor. Visibility was reduced to almost nil. We took a blow once we gained the stairs. We were trying to see and hear the whereabouts of the fire. The only sound we heard was that of chainsaws cutting away at the roof over our heads. The guys on the truck company were doing their thing to create a ventilation hole to give the tar-colored, carcinogenic smoke an exit.

George leaned his helmet into mine and shouted, "Let's wait until the trucks vents this place. We'll be able to see more in a minute." Good idea.

The truck crew completed its task and with the aid of a large fan at the front door, the smoke lifted and vision was restored. I looked down at the floor ahead of me. It was gone.

The fire had burned through from the main floor. A scant three feet more of crawling and gravity would have done its job on me. We worked the nozzle over a few hot spots around the flame-caused opening and went into mop-up mode.

When the fire was out, I thanked George for his wisdom and patience. I also bought him dinner, dessert and lots of doughnuts. It was the least I could do. After all, he prevented me from taking the express train to the ground floor. At best, I would have been singed and broken. At worst, I would have been history.

I plowed past the "Welcome to South Dakota" sign featuring those four dudes of Mount Rushmore fame. Below the picture was the slogan: "Great Faces, Great Places." This all sounded fine by me. The rural landscape was dominated once again by soybeans and corn. The roads were devoid of unpleasant things like chuckholes, cracks or traffic. Once again, I was smiling a lot.

At mile 75, I decided that it was time to call it a day and pulled into Canton. In 1867, the inhabitants gave the town the name it their belief that its position on the earth was directly opposite the Canton found in China. I guess places have been named for weirder reasons – maybe.

Another claim to questionable fame for Canton was being the site of the country's sole Asylum for Insane American Indians. This highly politically incorrect institution ran its course from 1903 to 1934. It was justifiably shuttered amid complaints of poor management and patient abuse.

Everyone seemed to be normal enough in this town of 3,000. In fact, it almost felt like a step back in time to the no-stress days of "Leave it to Beaver"-type normal. When I shopped at the supermarket, teenagers wearing white shirts, ties and aprons used such long-forgotten terms as, "thank you," "sir" and "ma'am," and my personal favorite, "please." The experience left me a badly shaken. Luckily, I recovered enough to get a restful night's sleep in this pleasant prairie town.

The next day was a wind-assisted mellow jaunt to Sioux Falls. I wanted to get there early to loosen up my arm for my 2009 pitching debut.

Emily from the misnamed Sioux Falls Canaries (that frail yellow warbler would never be able to survive a South Dakota winter) heard about my ride when I inquired about scoring a free ticket for a game. She politely asked me to drop by the ballpark to see if I would be interested in a proposition. I informed her I'd be able to fit the meeting into my busy schedule.

I met Emily, whose official title was director of promotions, at the stadium. She was a recent college graduate and a nestling in the Canaries organization. She came right to the point: "How would you like to ride your bike onto the ballpark and then throw out the first pitch? We'll give you a few tickets, too."

I was able to make my decision without even speaking to my agent: "Sign me up!"

I was left with a couple of hours to explore Sioux Falls' attractive downtown before game time. Here was a city that seemed to have sidestepped the nation's recent economic freefall. South Dakota's largest city boasted a low unemployment figure and a below-average cost of living. I did happen to hear some grumbling among residents concerning the low pay scale. The main industries are health care and banking, an odd couple. Then again, maybe not.

I looked at my watch and realized it was time to fly back to Canaries Stadium, also known as the Cage. I made a bullpen stop at nearby Nutty's for the pre-game ritual of stretching my pitching arm. My manager (me) told me it was OK to throw down a sandwich and accompanying Fat Tire beers before my big moment on the mound. A ballplayer needs to be properly hydrated.

I made my big entrance through a centerfield gate and followed the warning track to the El Paso Diablos' dugout. I parked my steed and jogged to the mound. I leaned in for the sign from the catcher, reared back and threw nothing but heat. Not exactly, but I like the way it sounds.

Regrettably, no agents jumped out of the stands to sign me up for the big leagues, so I returned to my bike. There I got a chance to banter with a couple of Diablos. They were well-mannered demons who seemed to be genuinely interested in my journey. I never got the chance to ask them any baseball-related questions. When the players heard the first strains of the National Anthem, the shucking and jiving ceased. They put on their game faces.

After standing at attention with my baseball cap respectfully behind my back, I retreated to my seat in the stands. It was time for me to watch real talent.

The Friday night crowd was enthusiastic as it cheered the Canaries, who edged the Texans 4-3. Let it be known that there was no mention of my pitching performance in the box score. Apparently, I was a fly-by-night sensation.

From Sioux Falls, I emigrated east back to Iowa on a potentially cruddy, cloudy Saturday morning. I was on a mission. I couldn't resist the pull of Iowa's tallest peak: Hawkeye Point was within my reach!

Interlude Back into Iowa

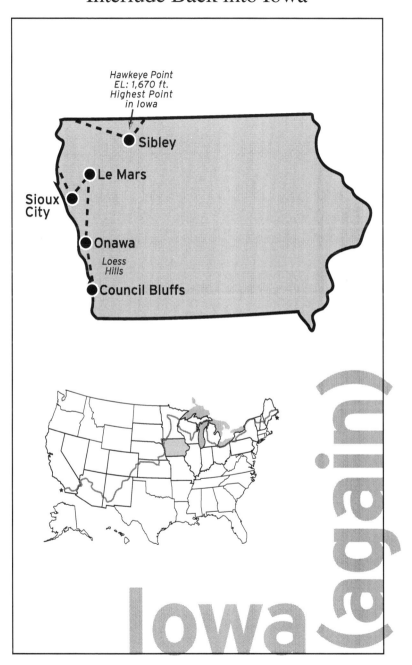

Hawkeye Point
EL: 1,670 ft.
Highest Point
in Iowa

Sibley

Le Mars

Sioux City

Onawa

Loess Hills

Council Bluffs

Iowa (again)

9. Interlude Back into Iowa

A 25-mph tailwind blew me effortlessly into Sibley, where I planned to bivouac for the night before my summit attempt.

After a restful night's sleep in another unremarkable Super 8 motel, I was ready to take on the challenge. I had recovered enough from my ordeal on Kansas' mighty Mount Sunflower to go for it. It was a heavy-metal wind that morning, with no storm clouds in sight. I figured, "What the hell?" I'm sure Sir Edmund Hilary would have concurred.

Hawkeye Point is on the northeast outskirts of Sibley off Highway 60. The massif loomed above me from the road. I turned east and one-eighth of a mile later I was standing on top of Iowa's high side, which weighs in at a nose-bleed elevation of 1,670 feet.

Whew! What a view! From my lofty perch I saw acres and acres of soybeans – simply astonishing. I shot a few commemorative photos, but tweaked my back while hefting my steed for the summit photo, thus proving once again how dangerous an endeavor mountaineering really is. I limped over to the register, signed in and made my way down to thicker air.

A handful of miles later, I entered the ninth state of this journey – Minnesota.

Muddled Down in Minnesota

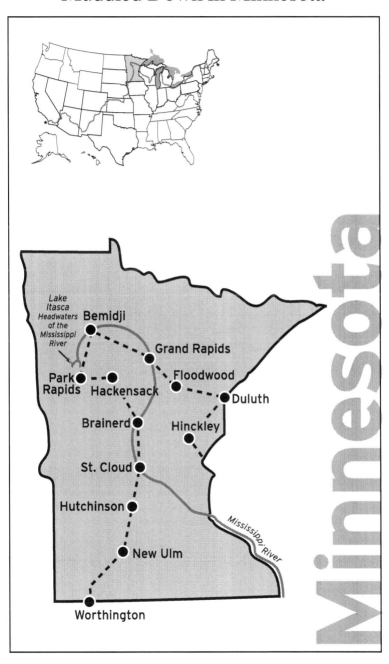

10. Muddled Down in Minnesota

It had been a quiet-up-to-that-point shift getting on to early evening when the tones sounded. "Engine Two! Westside ambulance! Report of a woman who jumped out the third floor window of Westfall Hall on campus. She is lying on the south side of the building."

We hustled over to the engine as the paramedics mounted their rig. With sirens screaming and emergency lights in overtime mode, it didn't take long for either unit to arrive on scene.

What we found there was too-much reality TV for most folks; a young woman face up in a pond of blood. A quick survey surprised us; she was still alive, but just barely. Amber liquid spurted out of her femoral artery, which was sliced by a shard of window glass. The lead paramedics applied pressure to the gaping wound and called out orders. "Jeff! Set up two IV bags of Ringer's. Brad! Get the backboard and cot. We need to move."

Our boss, Randy, watched over the scene and kept the lines of communications open and clear.

Once inside the ambulance, the usual controlled havoc ramped up to warp speed. We interrupted the chaos to perform CPR for a moment or two. She had a wisp of life in her when we arrived at the hospital emergency room, where the doctors, nurses, techs, and clerks assumed control of the patient. We did our job. She arrived with a pulse, of sorts.

A few weeks later, this suicidal patient was still alive and happy to be here. Shortly thereafter, she walked into Station Two while we were on duty. The same Westside ambulance crew was there as well.

She was a blond, pleasing-to-the-eye college coed with a shy smile.

"I'd like to thank you all for saving my life," she said.

Then she pointed at Mike the paramedic and said, "I remember your bald spot while I was looking down at all of you. I think you were doing CPR on me."

Whew! This was a real out-of-body experience. Apparently her chips had not been cashed in for her allotted time on Earth.

I felt proud and pleased that we were of assistance and wished her well. I believed she got the lesson that life really is a gift.

The site of a "Welcome to Minnesota" sign greeted me next door to an official state visitor center. There were a few other signs stating fun factoids about this northern state.

Did you know there are 15,000 lakes in the Gopher State? (The Minnesota license plate shorts the state 5,000 bodies of wetness.) There are 65 towns with "lake" in their names and there are 13 "falls," 10 "rivers", five "rapids" and a flood of beaches, bays and isles as part of their names. The state's name means "sky-colored water" in the Dakota language. Obviously, Minnesotans have water on their brains.

After reading all of that, I half expected to look down and be standing in water. But I only noticed the gone-postal winds. Then again, I should have known something was up. Wind-turbine farms sprouted from the flat fields like over-fertilized corn. The fan-look-alikes were everywhere.

At least on this day, the blast of air was friendly and on my back as it blew me into Windom.

I did a reconnoiter lap through downtown; most businesses were closed for the Christian Sabbath. I felt the pangs of an uneventful evening heading my way.

Later, while killing time in my hotel room, I read the latest issue of the Cottonwood County Citizen. In the letters to the editor section, a local voiced his strong opinion concerning a "fat, obnoxious black woman." I was pretty shocked to see the Citizen had printed such a nasty letter in such a genteel town.

Let the record show that Windom won the award for dullest overnight stop of my journey up to that point. The old joke, "I spent a week in Windom one day," came to mind. Maybe I need to write a letter to the editor about that.

The next day I escaped the ho-hum to seek out roads less traveled. The scene was corn, soy, wind farms and not much to photograph.

I ventured into Butterfield (population 564) with a dream of eggs-over-easy. Instead, I met Agnes.

This turned out to be a good thing. I chanced upon this gray-haired grandma when I asked her if Butterfield had any breakfast cafés. The answer was not what I hoped for.

"No, we don't, although the gas station does sell hot dogs and nachos!"

I had to admonish her: "Didn't your mother tell you that breakfast is the most important meal of the day? One shouldn't put junk food into one's temple!"

She got a chuckle out of that. Soon we were chatting away like old cronies.

"This town used to be booming. We even had railroad passenger service. Now the young people are moving away because there are no jobs," she said.

I asked her who the town's main employer was between bites of the cookies she had generously handed me.

"We have one chicken-processing plant. If they close down, Butterfield will be done."

How sad to think a town's fate is dependent on processed poultry.

I had many windy miles ahead of me before my day would terminate in New Ulm. It was time for me to go, so I said thanks and goodbye to this kindly matron.

"I'll make you a PB&J sandwich for your ride. It's a long way to New Ulm from here. Would you like wheat or white bread?"

There may only be 564 inhabitants in Butterfield, but I was glad one of them was Agnes.

I rode into the wind and off frantic Highway 60 and onto relaxed County Road 13. On my right I read a homemade sign proclaiming: "Rogan, Minnesota – ten people, three dogs and one cat." I never got a visual on any of the occupants as I lugged through the "town." I was fortunate to have pushed through before rush hour.

When I hit state Highway 15N en route to New Ulm, a crazed gale struck me face-first. One insane gust literally stopped me in mid-pedal – a rarity. It took me 2.5 hours to cover the last 18 miles. This was certainly no land-speed record, but the wind-turbine farms weren't complaining.

By the time I arrived in New Ulm, I was spent enough to require a nap before wandering downtown.

New Ulm was founded on the banks of the Minnesota River by German immigrants in the 1850s. The Teutonic influence is still evident in its old buildings and the neat and well-maintained homes and gardens. Everything is in its place and there's a place for everything. What else could one expect from the country that brought the world BMWs?

Downtown sported many German-named restaurants, a multitude of shops and, best of all, plenty of bars serving up locally made Schell beer. I took a foam break at the B and L Bar, where there were plenty of blond-haired, blue-eyed patrons with amble beer bellies. Here was living proof that the residents had not strayed too far from the Fatherland.

Yep, I surely enjoyed my evening in New Ulm heaps more than (yawn) Windom.

The next day I hit it early for my passage to Hutchinson and to beat the incessant winds. It didn't matter. After passing the "Auf Wiedersehen" sign at the edge of town, I proved that Kwik-Trip coffee was no match for the triple-espresso northerly winds. It was a lesson in futility as it took me five hours and then some to cover a mere 45 miles. If every day were this brutal, I'd still be in California.

In Hutchinson (Minnesota's hometown) the no-tell motel was already booked. I decided to open my wallet wider and splurge for an upgrade. My mind and body were trying to tell me something. I was tired. I splurged for an AmericInn. The clean and cozy room was the pampering I needed.

I relaxed before heading back to town for a meal and entertainment. At least I was able to find a meal. Las Vegas is not losing sleep about Hutchinson taking over the adult-entertainment arena.

I called it an early night while hoping that the "blow" would subside. I woke and peeked out the window to discover potential dreariness mixed with a bothersome breeze. I fueled up on a mega-dose of coffee and carbs for the impending onslaught.

At mile 15 on Highway 15, my eyes beheld my first Minnesota lake. It was no Great Lake and the name indicated that – Pigeon. By this point I was beginning to have my doubts about those 15,000 lakes. That was one down and 14,999 to go. Despite being a puddle, the lake yielded a flock of pelicans circling gracefully overhead. I never associated pelicans with Minnesota. I wondered whether the state issued hunting licenses for a pelican season.

I passed two more named lakes as the rest of the scenery was soy, corn, wheat and an occasional wind-whipped, bent-over tree.

Once in busy St. Cloud, I dodged the many RVs dragging boats to one of those 15,000 lakes. It was the start the Fourth of July pilgrimage to the great Minnesota Northwoods and I was in the middle of it.

After checking into another white-bread hotel, I took a stroll to see an old friend – the Mississippi River. En route I passed through the mostly shuttered downtown. There were too-numerous-to-count signs stating "Business for sale" and "Lease now" displayed in the doors and windows of empty storefronts. Even the low-rent bars seemed to be down on their luck.

For me, a glance at the Mississippi made up for the economic plight of St. Cloud. The river was still in its developmental stage, yet I stared at it in awe. I had made it to the Mighty Miss in less than two months and 3,000-plus miles. I felt pretty giddy.

I retreated uptown to the Granite City (St. Cloud's nickname) Brewery for an early dinner and happy hour. Soon I went to bed to pacify my weary body.

From St. Cloud I headed to Brainerd for a Fourth of July weekend break. I had not taken a day off the bike since Lincoln, Neb. I was feeling beat and thumped upon by an invisible force that causes "stop" signs to wobble and makes birds think twice about taking flight. I had to face the facts; the wind just doesn't play fair.

Bob and Jeanne Larson would be my hosts for the long weekend of R&R. The Larsons are a social and entertaining couple who I've known from the cycling community for years. They live in an old church. I would be truly heaven-blessed by staying there.

Following Bob's suggestions, I found serene roads that took me past the not-so-booming farming communities of Buckman, Genola, Pierz, and Freedham. The farther north I pedaled the wilder and less-tilled the land became. One of the few highlights was witnessing an aerial "dogfight" in which a few runty red-winged blackbirds chased away a fearful bald eagle. That's some national symbol of courage.

A few miles south of Brainerd I met Bob and Jeanne, who had biked out to show me the way to their home/church.

Bob, a retired photographer, and Jeanne, a retired kindergarten teacher, were almost as happy to see me as I was to see them. This fun-loving, gregarious couple has the reputation of ignoring Central Standard Time. They utilize a time zone of their own: Larson Time. This might mean breakfast is closer to the usual lunchtime and dinner could be to a midnight snack. I was determined to go with the flow, so I took off my watch.

The Brainerd area was first seen by a non-native in 1805, when that get-around-guy Zebulon Pike came through on an unsuccessful quest to discover the headwaters of the Mississippi River. I'm sure he wasn't thinking "Great American Desert" as he negotiated the thick underbrush and dense forests.

These days, this once big-time logging and railroad hub is all about the tourists. With that in mind, I played the part by eating, drinking and relaxing in excess during our nation's birthday weekend.

I did interrupt the sloth-like lifestyle to jog a 5-kilometer Fourth of July race sponsored by the Larsons. The event had a quirky name indicative of the organizers: Feet for Fools. Jeanne starred as the mistress of ceremonies. She admonished the eager crowd to "pay attention" as she shouted out instructions. Once a teacher, always a teacher.

After three nights of hardly thinking about my bike, it was time to get back to business. Jeanne volunteered to pedal with me out of town along a converted rail-to-trail multi-purpose route named after Paul Bunyan. Yes, I was in the land of that legendary woodsman and the locals were keen to cash in on it. Statues of Paul Bunyan and Babe the Blue Ox appeared at many towns' visitor centers. Just off the trail in Pine River, I took a photo of his oversized boots. Paul was just about everywhere in the great Northwoods.

Jeanne produced a steady stream of banter on as we rode the asphalt path and the miles melted away. Is this what happens when one rides with company?

After parting ways with Jeanne, I met up with Larry, the first bicyclist carrying gear I had met since Jay outside of Lincoln.

Larry wasn't on a point-A-to-point-B type of ride. His address was his bike. He had no final destination for his journey and his riding outfit looked more in line with custodial work than bicycle touring. He wore work boots to match his navy blue pants. His tent was of a heavy, canvas variety.

"I've been on my bike for three years now. I spend my time in the northern states in the summer and Texas in the winter," he said between pulls on a cigarette.

He went on to tell me not to fret about money since, "We'll be having the second Civil War soon. Money won't mean anything. That's why I need to maintain my Texas state citizenship. They will be the first to secede."

After he began to sprinkle his conversation with the "N" word and other derogatory terms for fellow humans, I had enough of Larry. I might be a tad crazy, but I'm not nuts. I don't recall wishing him a safe journey.

I returned to the peace of the Paul Bunyan Trail, which became quite rural between Backus and Hackensack. It was almost a shame to be done for the day.

In Hackensack (why would anyone name a town after someplace in New Jersey?) I secured a room in the Owl's Nest hotel. Its motto: "We give a hoot!"

After a quick lap around Hackensack that took three minutes, I came across Paul B's significant other. The ever-enticing Lucette guarded the pier and park adjacent to Birch Lake. Maybe "ever-enticing" is an exaggeration. Homely would have been more accurate for this 17-foot-tall creation of wood, paint and cement. Alas, in Paul's eyes she was a babe, and not the blue ox kind. Close by was their prodigy, Paul Junior, who was born – or should I say carved – four decades later. The tyke apparently was a mama's boy who didn't stray far from Lucette's large apron.

For Happy Hour I ventured into Lucette's Pizza and Pub. While sipping a cold frosty, I noticed four bullet holes in the plate glass windows. I guess people get highly agitated about lax service in this neck of the Northwoods.

I discovered later that an irate boyfriend of a waitress shot up the joint. The hard-nosed bartender went on to say, "The freaking local cop was too busy donning his bullet-proof vest to get the bastard!" Her story got more interesting. "After that incident, the town disbanded the police department as a way to get rid of that cop. Come to think about it, we have less crime now, too."

Maybe there is a lesson here.

That evening I had a surprise guest arrive. Kathy from Albuquerque was back in her home state for a friends-and-family visit. She was gracious enough to include me in her schedule. Once again I found myself part of a temporary couple. We caught up on each other's lives and other things.

In the morning, we made a plan to meet in nearby Park Rapids. She had grownup matters to attend to, like work and phone calls. I had my biking job to deal with.

I regained the Paul Bunyan Trail heading north and into Chippewa National Forest. In this secluded section it seemed as if I were backpacking upon a bicycle. The solitude was broken by a handful of dirt roads and one loon plying the waters of a minor lake. It was all pretty sweet.

The Paul Bunyan Trail eventually gave way to the Heartland Trail. In Akeley, a larger-than-life statue of Paul B. stood adjacent to Highway 34. He was so colossal I sat comfortably in his outstretched palm. His ax dwarfed my bike. I was beginning to believe the tall tales about that legendary woodsman.

In Nevis, I took a moment to cast a glance at the world's largest tiger muskellunge statue. This was one fish that didn't get away. Minnesotans certainly like their roadside attractions to be overstated.

I breezed into Park Rapids with a tailwind for a change. After collecting Kathy and a hug, we set off for Itasca State Park.

Minnesota's first state park was established in 1891 and is best known for containing the headwaters of the Mississippi River.

The source of the 2,552-mile waterway was a much sought-after prize. In 1832, a helpful Indian guide led Henry Rowe Schoolcraft past bogs, lakes and lots of timber to this sacred spot. Schoolcraft came up with a catchy name for the lake from which the infantile Mississippi oozes – Itasca. He melded two Latin words meaning "truth" and "head." He must have been thinking "tourist attraction." Barnum and Bailey would have been proud of this showman.

Hordes of geography buffs (like me), tourists and families venture to northern Minnesota to walk, slide or swim across the not-so-mighty river. Kathy and I were no exception. We even shot photos to prove it.

It might not have been a wilderness experience, but seeing those water-logged kiddies, their happy parents and enthusiastic spectators made for an enjoyable time. It was a pleasant outing for Minnesota's newest temporary couple as well.

The following morning my tummy hurt and I felt beaten down. This was no "love bug." I had run afoul of a Brainerd belly-bloat malady. Many of Jeanne and Bob's weekend guests arrived ill that Fourth of July weekend, and apparently I had picked up the virus.

After saying a proper farewell to Kathy, it was time to depart. Once again, I was a solo traveler. (I found out later that Kathy managed to stay healthy.)

The weather cooperated for my return trip to Itasca via bicycle. It would not have been right to deny my faithful steed the privilege of seeing this landmark. It was déjà vu all over again except seeing a lone black bear cross in front of me. Another Animal Planet moment was lost due to a stowed camera.

I exited Itasca State Park and followed signs for the Great River Road as I crisscrossed the embryonic mighty Mississippi. The river was a meandering stream with ox bows, grassy bottoms and see-through water, a far cry from what it looks like 2,552 miles to the south. Except for the gurgling sound emitting from my gut, all was quiet on the Great River Road.

I arrived in Bemidji, which happens to be the first city on the Mississippi. Here the waterway has an identity problem: Is it a chain of lakes or a river? Apparently the decision on whether to be a lake/river had been placed on hold for the time being.

Bemidji Lake has a river inlet on its west side and an outlet on its east side. A visitor center occupies the western lakeshore. Surprise! Paul Bunyan and Babe the Blue Ox are present and accounted for.

According to legend, Paul was born in Bemidji. The Paul and Babe statues were weak sisters compared to Akeley's. A gerbil would barely fit into Paul's palm. As far as Babe goes, I've seen Great Danes that were more impressive in size. I can play the tall-tale game, too.

After spending the evening in low-profile mode, I felt somewhat better prior to a planned 80-mile endeavor to Grand Rapids. Of course, I woke to headwinds.

I headed out on the Great River Road again as it attempted to shadow the waterway. Each time I saw the river, I noticed an added volume of water to offset the decreased clarity. By the time I made U.S. Highway 2, it became apparent what had happened out of my eyesight. The river had been dammed upstream. The telltale "bathtub ring" on the sandbars was the evidence. The Mississippi was running wild no more.

A stone's throw from Grand Rapids was a Corps of Engineer's dam followed by another blockage at the Blandin paper mill. There were no rapids in Grand Rapids. The river had been tamed and controlled.

I stopped in at the visitor center and met Nira, a 75-year-old volunteer who doled out basic Grand Rapids information (Birthplace of Judy Garland; no yellow brick road in sight.) and an array of strong opinions. She made it known that these were her thoughts and not the official Grand Rapids party line.

"Our high school was forced to change its name from the Indians to the Thunderhawks. What's a Thunderhawk? We got along so well with our Indians. What's all the fuss about?" she fumed.

She then added wistfully, "Our prom queen wore a magnificent feathered headdress. It's all gone."

I defused her a bit when I asked if she was a recent prom queen. That wisecrack had the desired effect. Nira's blood pressure went down a notch.

I woke not feeling quite right, again. A tree-swaying headwind didn't improve my condition. I was beginning to think that the true meaning of the word Minnesota was "freaking windy place." I decided to cut my losses with a short 38-mile ride to Floodwood. I made my departure from the Great River Road with a twinge of regret.

The scenery matched my mood; desolate and boggy. Vegetation was sparse and made up of stunted or dead spruce trees. Maybe the wind killed them.

The town of Floodwood was ramping up for the weekend Catfish Festival. After all, every Minnesotan knows Floodwood is the Catfish Capital of the state. If you need a reminder, it is written on the town's water tower.

In one bar I read the schedule of events: street dance, 5-K run, cow-pie throwing contest, basketball tournament, wrestling matches, pancake breakfast, catfish fishing contest and the inevitable beer garden. On Sunday, the beer garden began operating at the same time as the outdoor church service. Take your choice; holy water vs. bubbly water. I like a town that offers options.

Before moseying toward Duluth, my icky stomach needed sustenance. I walked into the Bridgeman's Café, where ample-sized local men took the counter seats, so I settled into a booth. I eavesdropped as the topics of conversation flowed with the coffee. The talk was about the Catfish Festival, the latest economic stimulus package, mud bog races, Sven's $250 Social Security raise (he had to buy a round of coffee for the gaggle) and a road-paving crew that recently hired a few women.

The storyteller continued: "One already called in sick because it was her period. It'll be like clockwork from now on." An uncomfortable silence followed as those gentlemen digested the remark. The topic of conversation was quickly changed.

I left the homespun philosophers for Duluth, a municipality once described as the "zenith city of unsalted waters." As usual, the wind

157

got going before I did. As unusual, it was on my back, praise the Lord. My bicycle felt like it had an engine on it for 46 miles.

Halfway there I crossed over Highway 2 to jaw with PJ, another cross-country rider. It was his turn to suffer into the wind. He was long and lanky and sported a rough-and-tumble beard that made him look older than his 23 years. His story went like so: "I graduated Plymouth College a few weeks ago, so I figured what the heck? My student loans won't come due until December."

It's hard to argue with reasoning like that. Young people like PJ give me hope for the future generations. After exchanging road and town information, we both proceeded on.

I crested a final hill past the "Sarah Palin in 2012" sign (I tried to ignore it) and saw Lake Superior, a full-fledged natural wonder if there ever was one.

Here are a few fun factoids about this watery marvel: It's the largest lake in the world in terms of area, it contains one-tenth of all the freshwater on the globe, and if its waters were spread out over North and South America, we would all be wading through its one-foot depth. Now that's a lake.

A decade had passed since I last visited Duluth. Back then I used it as the starting point for a 1,300-mile circumnavigation bike tour around Lake Superior. Like an old friend, it was good to see Duluth and the lake again.

I met distant acquaintances Rob and Brenda Brannan on their lunch break downtown on Superior Street. They surprised me with a gift certificate they had won in a raffle for a hotel room at the Inn on Lake Superior. After a quick bite, they returned to making money and I checked into my lakeside pad. The room was immaculate and tastefully decorated. It had scented lotions and a flat screen TV. Best of all, the patio was so close to the lake, I could practically fish from it. So this is what it felt like to be a VIP.

After reveling in the luxury, I took a stroll around Canal Park for a round of sight-seeing. I picked up a copy of the Duluth "Shipping News" to get a read on the local entertainment schedule. One of Duluth's biggest tourist attractions is watching behemoth freighters cruise under the aptly named Aerial Lift Bridge.

Duluth is the end point of the St. Lawrence Seaway. Ocean- and Great Lakes-going vessels enter the harbor to load up on grain, coal and taconite pellets (iron ore.) A new guy on the block is imported European wind turbines meant to feed America's insatiable energy appetite. Wind in the Midwest? I hadn't noticed.

After glancing at the shipping "rap" sheet, I was surprised by the lack of freighters making landfall. In 1999, the ships were queued up like kids waiting to sit on a department-store Santa's lap. I took this as another sign of the world's mired-down economy. Why move iron ore when there is no market for the Big Three's Chevy Blazers, Ford Explorers or Dodge Mini-vans?

With a still-queasy gut, I met the Brannans for dinner and drinks. They are an embedded couple in Duluth. They raised their three children here and were going through the pangs of being empty nesters.

Rob manages to take advantage of the lake. He's been known to ice-fish it during the long winters and canoe on it during the short summers. Brenda seems content to just look at its sublime beauty.

I picked up the tab after the oh-so-generous gift certificate they gave me. It was close to my sleepy time when we said our good nights. I was walking back to my opulent hotel room when my cell phone rang. It was Brenda: "There's a freighter coming into the harbor. If you hurry you can see it at the bridge." The race was on.

I barely beat the 1,000-foot-long Edgar B. Speer's arrival to inhale a load of taconite. A sizable crowd awaited the ship's arrival. The crew must have felt like rock stars as they waved to admirers. It was quite evident there would be no autograph session. I went to bed ship-satisfied.

After taking breakfast on my lakeside patio, I found the Willard Munger State Trail south of Duluth. This long-distance trail is named in honor of the longest-serving member of the Minnesota House of Representatives. Mr. Munger, who served 42 years, 7 months, before his death in 1999, apparently was "green" before it was cool. The trail guide summed it up well: "We are all his beneficiaries."

The trail ascended a ridge overlooking Lake Superior; the views were splendid. The trail was laid over an old railroad track. The grades were gentle, which was just fine for my fatigued body. A few miles into my ride, I passed a couple of runners with numbers pinned to their shorts. Turned out I was pedaling in the middle of a trail-run marathon. The endurance athletes looked fresher than I felt. When I crossed the finish line, good-natured volunteers cheered me on and handed me cookies and water as if I were a participant. They must have really put on a show when an actual runner comes through.

I continued on the smooth-as-silk trail still devoid of cyclists. In Moose Lake, I took a lunch break in the old railroad depot/museum. It featured a somber presentation concerning the forest fire of 1918.

The inferno took the lives of 453 people in the surrounding area. A spark from a passing train set a sad scenario in motion. High winds, bone-dry conditions and slash piles left by loggers were the main ingredients for this quarter-million-acre fire. (No, it was not bigger than Rhode Island.) In total, 38 communities were destroyed. It was the worst natural disaster in Minnesota history.

With these sobering thoughts in mind, I arrived two hours later at the trail's termination in Hinckley, where I learned history does repeat itself. Hinckley was the site of a firestorm in 1898. A mass grave in the town's aptly named Memorial Park contains the remains of some of the 418 victims.

On this Saturday, the Corn and Clover Festival was making downtown a happening place. I arrived in time to see and hear the multi-media presentation of the Minnesota Brass, Drum and Bugle Corps in action. They featured a mob of musicians, dancers and baton twirlers. The earnest performers displayed a determined look. The band leader must have been a strict enforcer of the No Smiley Face rule. As far as the music goes, it had an OK beat, but could I dance to it?

I went to bed early, unconcerned about bands, conflagrations, corn or clover. I wanted to get plenty of Zs to feel healthy once again.

On a dank, misty cool morning, I made my exit from Minnesota. I crossed over the St. Croix River and gained Wisconsin, "land of

161

industry, recreation and agriculture." That's what the welcome sign said, so it must be true.

Wandering in Wisconsin

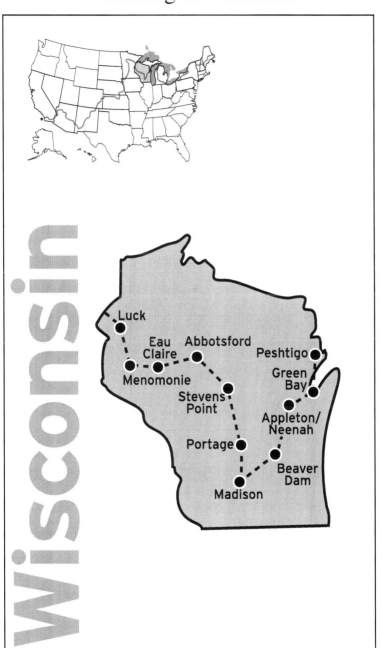

11. Wandering in Wisconsin

"Engine Two! Westside ambulance! Respond to a report of a car versus motor scooter accident at Colorado State University. Report of one patient with an injured leg …"

I was driving that day as we made our way across campus. With the ambulance riding in our slipstream we arrived on scene at the same time. The scene immediately struck me as odd since the attractive college coed we found was lying face up on the hood of the sedan that had struck her motor scooter. Patients usually slide off upon impact. But there she was; an alive-yet-injured hood ornament.

We went to work with a backboard, C-collar, IVs, O2 and a hare traction splint for the woman's apparently broken femur. I never uttered a word to her. I was assigned go-fer patrol: "Jeff! Go-fer this! Go-fer that!" The ambulance took her the hospital and our job was done.

About half a year later, a captain from another shift called me at home.

"Jeffy! We just did a fire inspection at a daycare center and the woman manager asked about you."

"Ralph! Don't jack with me. I haven't had a girlfriend in a while."

"No, seriously! She described you and said you were her hero when she was hit by a car on her motor scooter."

"You mean that attractive coed who was a hood ornament?"

"That's the one!"

I got up the nerve to call the daycare center a few days later.

"Hello! My name is Jeff. Are you the woman who had the motor scooter accident at CSU?"

"Yes!"

"Well, I am one of the guys who showed up on that call. Are you OK?"

"I'm doing well, thank you. My name is Tasha. You are my hero."

Only Hollywood could have scripted this scenario. I ended up dating the ever-enticing Tasha more than a year. Ultimately, my lack of desire for the "C" word (commitment), which might lead to the "M" word (marriage), led to our relationship's demise.

Almost to the day we broke up, she introduced me as her hero. Once in awhile being a firefighter had side benefits.

The moment I crossed into the state of beer, brats and cheese, I felt healthier. My history of riding in Wisconsin goes back more than 20 years. I can honestly say I've never had a bad visit to the "Badger State." Then again, a state that once considered the slogan "Come and Smell our Dairy Air" as an advertising gimmick is my kind of place.

Highway 70 was packed with Minnesota "Gophers" towing campers and boats back west to the Twin Cities. The majority of those weekend fishermen had their Sunday game faces on in preparation for another week in the cubicle. I smiled despite the sloppy weather at the thought of my wonderful schedule. Every day was a weekend.

I eased off the main highway and onto County Road W and quickly became reacquainted with the wonders of Wisconsin cycling. The road curled, dipped and swirled through a landscape of farmland, cows and wooded lots filled with majestic white pines that were lucky enough to have escaped the ax-men. This was truly Midwest cycling nirvana.

In Frederic, I spent the equivalent of one beer to ride the Gandy Dancer State Recreational Trail. This rail trail is named in honor of the railroad crews that maintained the tracks. The hand tools of choice were made by the Gandy Tool Co. of Chicago. The 98-mile route follows the old Minneapolis, St. Paul and Sault St. Marie line from St. Croix Falls to Superior. I suppose the powers to be must have dug deep to come up with the unusual name.

After six miles of crunching limestone, I was in Luck – Wisconsin, that is.

When I spied this dot on the map, it only seemed right to spend a night in Luck. The rural legend reads like this: If you arrived near Butterfield Lake by nightfall after a day's wagon ride from Sioux Falls, you were in luck!

Loggers and Danes filled the town site. Many years later, Duncan Yo-Yos produced its wares from the local forest products until it was bought out. Duncan made great tops, too.

I spent a mellow Sunday evening walking around downtown. A sign announced the upcoming Lucky Days Festival. I was out of Luck; I'd miss the party by one week.

Between a few beers and a meal, I picked up two Powerball lottery tickets. I reckoned I was in Luck and destined to win. The woman at the convenience store said, "We sell lots of lottery tickets for a town this tiny." In other words, a multitude of folks bought tickets in Luck thinking they, too, were destined to win. I ended up making 15 bucks from one of those tickets. Not enough to free me of money worries, but better than zilch.

That night I slept well for the first time in more than a week. I even had an appetite when I awoke. My gut crud had finally run its course. Perhaps I needed a new state to get me right.

I continued in a southerly direction on the Gandy Dancer Trail, scaring up cottontail rabbits and white-tail deer along the route to St. Croix Falls. It was a good-to-be-alive, blue-sky day with an autumn crispness to the air. I checked my cell phone for the date – July 13. Where did summer go?

I spent the day shadowing the wild and scenic St. Croix River, a waterway that achieved national park status for its beauty and historical significance. It was pretty impressive stuff, for the Midwest.

I stopped in Somerset to take on a second breakfast. There I met newbie bike tourists Ken and Jill from Rochester, Minn. Jill was sporting a bright white knee brace: never a good sign. While they ate omelets and I consumed a Frisbee-sized pancake, I handed out encouragement and advice. In a nutshell it went like this: Pace yourself, granny gears are your friend and bike touring is supposed to be fun (most of the time.)

When Jill hobbled off to the restroom, I had a man-to-man chat with Ken.

"Do you want Jill to join you for your next tour?" I asked.

"Of course. We get along great."

"Then 86 the camping gear and lower your mileage. She is not into doing Tour de France distances with a full load."

"Think so? You might have a point there."

I never thought I would play Dr. Phil and dish advice about relationships and bicycle touring. I wonder when Oprah might be hiring again.

When Jill returned, I wished them good luck for their weeklong ride. I hoped it would not end in a premature break up.

I made my way past historic Hudson, which resides on the banks of the St. Croix River, and bought offerings of beer, coffee and dessert for my hosts that evening. Ernie and his wife, Patty, and his daughter Ella were bicycle enthusiasts who I met on the GRABAAWR, an organized bicycle tour in Wisconsin. It stands for the Great Annual Bicycle Adventure Along the Wisconsin River.

Through the wonders of email and mutual acquaintances, I scored an invite for dinner and a bed. But first I had to run the gauntlet of County Road F (as in freaking); this was a narrow, busy byway with no shoulder and an interstate's volume of traffic. Oh yeah, this poor excuse for a road had many miles of destruction – I mean construction – assaulting it as well.

I white-knuckled it for a few miles before the commuter traffic subsided and I was finally able to glance about at the landscape. The St. Croix River was to my right, but all the trees, farms and subdivisions obscured the view. In fact, I was still able to see Minnesota across the valley.

After 70 miles of forward progress, I arrived at Ernie and Patty's country estate. It had been more than decade since I last saw Ernie. In that time span, he got divorced, had a bout of cancer, remarried and fathered a child. He had been a lot busier than me from social and health standpoints. Despite all the ups and downs, Ernie was still the same old positive, can-do type of guy. His parents must have known how he would turn out – Earnest. Those experiences did not jade him in the least bit. Ernie is a survivor in the truest sense.

I could tell my normal bicycle tourist's appetite had returned. While eating dinner, the other guests (also GRABAAWR acquaintances) were careful to not place their fingers too close to my mouth. It seemed so long and so many miles ago since I experienced the sensation of hunger.

Between the entree and dessert, Ernie meticulously scrubbed down my steed. All that grime, grease and grit upset his high standards of bike maintenance. I think it made him almost ill to see it that way. After he was done, I barely recognized my metal buddy. Did you know bicycle chains are silver in color?

On a wet and gray morning, I got into hyper-dawdle mode knowing that I had an abbreviated day of riding ahead of me. The forecast was for improved conditions and worth the wait. Ernie played the perfect host by supplying me with unlimited food and coffee.

When the last moisture-bearing cloud went by and Ernie put on a business suit, it was time for me to go. Besides, watching someone go off to work made my stomach ache return. I could almost feel his pain. Almost.

Back at my job, I finally felt like my old self, whoever that is. For a change the miles drifted by with little or no effort en route to Menomonie.

It's a little known fact that in the 1870s, this town was home to the greatest lumber corporation in the world. The local college is named after a lumber baron from those bygone days – The University of Wisconsin-Stout (the man, not the beer.)

I didn't hear the buzz of chainsaws or cries of "Timber!" upon my arrival. I only noticed a drowsy, small-college town wedged between Lake Menomonie and the Red Cedar River.

I made it over to Skoogs Supper Club and motel on the edge of town for a room, maybe a stout and a meal – one-stop shopping for a cycling tourist if there ever was one. After paying the clerk, who was like Woody Harrelson's character from "Cheers," I checked out my home for the night.

WOW! Was I surprised! There was a full-sized mirror suspended over the bed. The love nest was adorned with blood-red covers, sheets and pillows, too. The hard-working, blue-collar folks of the Badger State must possess a kinky side to their seemingly quiet lives. I surmised one has to invent some unique bedroom activities during those long winter months. I tried not to giggle when I re-entered Skoogs for dinner and drinks.

Between bites of dinner, sips of beer and glancing at the NBA All-Star game on TV, I spoke to John. He was a 30-something, tattooed, chain smoker whose roots in Menomonie predate

Wisconsin becoming a state in 1848. He waxed on about his family's cemetery, historical artifacts and Captain Dan, who was in charge of 250 soldiers during the Civil War. John was unable to fill me in on what battles Captain Dan and his men fought in, but he was proud of him nevertheless.

"He made it through that war without getting injured."

Who knows, maybe Captain Dan ruled over 250 clerks and the worst injury might have been a nasty paper cut.

John's political views were somewhere between Fox News and the attitude, "America! Love it or leave it!" He didn't think much of all the newcomers entering our land, either. "They come here and try and bend America to their idea of what it should be."

I didn't feel the need to mention that both my parents came from Europe to escape Hitler's idea of the master race.

I switched the subject by asking him what he did for a living. "I'm a professional gambler. I play poker in the nearby Indian casinos. It keeps me in drink and smokes." He must have run out of luck because he was currently homeless. He was checked into Skoogs on that rainy evening. I wondered if he had a mirror over his bed.

When conversing with John became too tedious, my attention was drawn to a middle-age couple out for dinner and drinks. We struck up a conversation that soon turned to the inevitable "Mister, you're not from around here, are you?"

I gave them the Reader's Digest version of my trip. The gray-haired husband looked up from his whiskey and said, "You've got to be nuts!"

My answer was quick and to the point, "Maybe, but I'm not dangerous."

His wife took a slow sip of her gin and tonic and said, "I don't know, Hal, he might be the only sane one here!"

I woke with nary a kinky thought or dream and headed out for the 40 miles to Eau Claire. At a kiosk near a parking lot, I invested a few Georges to pay the toll for using the Red Cedar State Trail. Soon I realized it was money well spent. It was almost as satisfying as a cold beer on a muggy day.

The former railroad bed hugged the banks of the Red Cedar River. Lush hanging gardens clung to limestone cliffs. On the river, blue herons were fishing sans licenses. Two sandhill cranes pecked at the loamy earth of a plowed field. Human presence was low, which was a good thing.

For 15 miles I enjoyed the splendor of this jewel, but it wasn't over. I veered onto the Chippewa River State Trail for the remainder of my ride. The trail wasn't quite as intimate with wider views of a wider river. The route passed a smattering of former logging towns. Mother Nature hates a void. She filled in those communities with grass and young forests.

I discovered that bears must enjoy a view when they "go potty." There was an inordinate amount of bear scat on the bridges overlooking the waterways. The age-old question, "Does a bear shit in the woods?" has finally been answered. No! A bear would rather poop on a bridge.

I arrived in Eau Claire with plenty of time for R&R before the Eau Claire Express took on the Waterloo Bucks at Carson Field.

In the summer of 2008, I contrived a bicycle tour I dubbed the "Thirteen Ballparks and a Wedding Ride." A pal's nuptials provided me with an excuse to journey from Albany, N.Y., to Dubuque, Iowa, catching minor league ballgames along the way. That summer I had the pleasure of meeting Brett Schroedel, the young general manager of the Express. After telling him about my ride, he allowed me to heave the first pitch. (I bounced it in front of the plate.) In 2009, I wasn't as fortunate. Good ol' Brett remembered me and handed me a free ticket, but the honor of throwing out the ceremonial pitch went to a former major leaguer, Ron Coomer. (But can he ride a bike cross-country?)

Without the pressure of a pitching performance, I took some locals' advice and stopped into the Joynt Bar on Water Street. This was not a typical Wisconsin bar. There were no dead animals on the walls and neon beer signs were at a minimum. Instead of those ornaments, the bar had multitudes of black-and-white photos of old rock stars and posters of R. Crumb's Head Comix. Near the beer taps, a sign proclaimed, "NO LIGHT BEER!" For this patron, it was love at first sight. The 60-cent-beer Happy Hour might have added to the infatuation, too.

While I was chillin', sipping and reading the newspaper, my attention was drawn to a dog. The hound was not outside doing doggie things. This one was sitting brown belly-up to the bar on a stool. He had a beer glass in front of him and a grin. Skootch wasn't a barfly. He was the official Joynt Bar mascot, and quite the ladies pooch, too. I watched enviously as he leaned his muzzle into a coed's ear as if to whisper "Come here often?" Or maybe it was, "What's your sign?" I could tell I was in the presence of pure pub genius.

Eventually, I left the cozy sanctuary of the Joynt to take in a ballgame. Eau Claire is the baseball venue where an 18-year-old Henry Aaron jump-started his professional career. Do you think Hammerin' Hank stood out in the Midwestern sea of white folks and white bread? Now a bronze statue of Henry stands sentinel at the main gate of Carson Field.

The contest started off swell with a pair of ospreys soaring over the center field while the National Anthem played. Their nest was on top of an outfield light pole, so their kids could catch the game. During a lull in the action, I noticed papa osprey dropped by with a squirming fish for the kiddies. That's a good dad.

The crowd was entertained between innings with spaghetti-eating contests, marshmallow golf balls being stroked into the outfield, a tidy-whitey underwear race, a toilet paper toss, and a pint-sized batboy attempting to swing an adult sized bat. There was never a dull moment except for watching the Express get derailed 12-3 by the Bucks.

I awoke the next day to a fearful wind for my long-distance ride to Abbotsford. Lucky for me, I was moving due east while the breeze was shaking the trees from the west. I kept my head down and tried to ignore that invisible commotion creating havoc around me.

After a few northern twists on lonely roads, I stumbled onto County Road X and the historic Yellowstone Trail, a long-forgotten route (1912-1930) that spanned the northern tier states. At the time it was the only transcontinental route in these higher latitudes. The road was the brainchild of J.W. Parmley of Ipswich, S.D. He and his business buddies envisioned a "good road from Plymouth Rock to Puget Sound." They lobbied for good roads at every government level. Their efforts paid off for me as I headed east on a leftover section of the trail. This route might have gained more notoriety if John Steinbeck wrote about it. Then again, "Get your kicks on the Yellowstone Trail" doesn't exactly slide off the tongue.

I was wasted after the 75-mile ride to Abbotsford and spent a low-key night in my room. I even dined there. For me, that's tired.

The next morning, a record-setting cold day for July 17 greeted me. Oh, joy! I threaded my legs through cycling tights for the first time since leaving San Diego. I also donned a hat, gloves, two fleece shirts and a jacket to match my leggings. This was scary; I was wearing all of my cold-weather gear in July. Would I have to buy a down jacket and mukluks before Maine?

I rolled through Colby and the birthplace of Colby cheese. Once again, it must have been true since it was written on the town's water tower. The locals were gearing up for the upcoming Colby Cheese Days weekend. The weather didn't seem to be too conducive for eating orange cheese outside, although for those tough Wisconsin cheeseheads, the temperature probably was balmy.

From the world of cheese I quickly entered the world of ginseng. Near Marathon, self-proclaimed Ginseng Capital of the World, I saw acres and acres of shaded plots where the gnarly root grew below the dappled sunlight. Marathon ginseng growers produce more than a million pounds of the herb every year. This strange-looking root allegedly acts as an energizer, stress reducer and aphrodisiac for men and women. Most of it gets shipped to Hong Kong. I wonder if Chinese men consume less Viagra than their American counterparts.

I was en route to Mosinee (home of the paper company) to get reacquainted with two old friends: the Wisconsin River and Calvin.

My love affair with the Dairy State goes back into the early '80s when I signed on for the GRABAAWR, a lovely ride starting at the headwaters of the Wisconsin River running to its final plunge into the Mississippi River. Little did I know how many acquaintances I would harvest from one organized ride. Calvin was one of them. It was very appropriate to see him and his bike once again on the banks of the Wisconsin River.

Calvin is an understated and unassuming truck driver whose beer-and-bratwurst belly belies the fact that he is a gifted athlete. Besides being a strong bike rider, Calvin rates "first wave" status in the Birkebeiner cross-country ski race, which is North America's largest ski race. With his "Aw, shucks!" disposition, I would rate him a first-wave character as well.

We rode and talked our way to Stevens Point, where I secured another cheap yet clean room. We met Mikey at a nearby watering hole for Happy Hour and a few pitchers and snacks. The afternoon slid into the evening as the beers went down way too easy. By 9:30 p.m., I was toast. Mikey and Calvin then announced that they would join me for the first 50 miles of my next day's ride. Even in the inebriated state I was in, I thought, "Yeah, right!"

Needless to say, there was no early morning phone call from those lads, just an early morning hangover for me. The business of biking cross-country doesn't understand a headache or nausea; it was still a travel day for me. Besides, I had a three-night layover in Madison acting like the proverbial carrot on a stick. I was motivated to de-bike in that college town.

Off I headed wearing my complete wardrobe once again. There wasn't a hint of blue sky, just black-and-white TV gray. It seemed fitting with my state of mind. My game plan was to go long to Portage, which would set me up for a short cruise into Madison and R&R. All I had to do was stay on the bike for untold hours.

I stalked the side roads closest to I-39 to avoid bonus miles en route to Portage. The alphabet of Wisconsin roads rolled by as my odometer marched on. Road V veered into CH, which morphed into M, which turned into CX and a Big Truck Mud-Race Festival in Endeavor. The "Big Foot" truck drivers hardly noticed me from their lofty perches. I felt insignificant and like an insect as they lumbered by.

Once in Portage, I eased through the newer north side, through the historic downtown and past the Wisconsin River levees in search of the Lamp-Lite Motel. On my Yahoo search for accommodations, one misguided review stated "clean and nice" (it wasn't) and close to downtown (2.5 miles is close for nuclear weapons.)

After 87 miles of motion, I arrived. The 1950s art deco sign was missing a letter or two. Weeds and Chinese elms sprouted up across the sparse excuse for a lawn. Exhausted pop machines, cigarette dispensers, refrigerators and a locked up (yet disconnected) ice machine provided the outside décor. Discarded car and truck seats, complete with seatbelt attachments in case of an earthquake, were in vogue as patio furniture. On a positive note, I was the lone occupant.

Marauding bands of Hell's Angels would bypass this joint as being too chancy.

I checked in with Ed in an office teeming with multiple generations of clutter. He made a show of calling housekeeping to see which room had received the "deodorizer machine" treatment. The phone line was dead. There was no housekeeping.

"I think room No. 2 is all spruced up and ready," he said.

I hauled out my credit card to pay $39 for the room. Surprise! The credit card machine was down. I laid the cash on his chaos of a desk while he made out a hand-written receipt. On it he wrote, "No refunds!" twice and underlined it. This was getting creepier by the second.

I opened the door to No. 2 and was struck by the stench of mold, dust, cigarette smoke, age and a strange odor of human activities. The air was so stale I doubted there was enough oxygen to sustain a match.

Dark wood paneling that was popular in the '60s, a calendar (right year, at least) and a few cheap paintings gave the room a homey feel – not!

The towels were the color of wet sand. I believe there was a time when they were white. I was beginning to understand the "No refund" policy. This sucker (me) was caught, hook, line and sinker.

At least I was able to walk to the Rathskeller Bar and Grill from the Lamp-Lite. Location, location, location.

The smoky bar was a welcome reprieve from my dingy room. The $1.50 microbrews on tap and a fresh newspaper provided a warm welcome. The friendly bartender asked me if I was passing through.

When I told her the sad truth about where I was staying, she said matter-of-factly, "Oh, the Bates Motel! No one has ever been murdered there, though!" I hoped I would not be the first.

After a surprisingly good night's sleep, I showered while keeping a watchful eye on the stained curtain. I never turned my back to the door. After a quick dry off, I escaped to Madison.

Sunday morning traffic was sleep-in light as I followed Highway 51 and roads VJ, J and other assorted numbers and letters to Lodi. Yes, the very same Lodi famous for being home of "Suzie the Duck." The nickname is in honor of the so-called wild ducks that always nest in a stone basket adjacent to Spring Creek. Since 1948, the nesting mom has been named "Suzie."

I stopped at the creek where three ducks were sleeping away, their bills tucked beneath their wings. It must have been a flight-of-fancy Saturday night for them. Not one responded to "Suzie" when I called.

I was saddened to learn I would miss "Suzie the Duck Days" by three weeks. Rats!

On the outskirts of Lodi, I gazed at three sandhill cranes browsing in a farmer's field. They reminded me that I was close to Baraboo and the International Crane Foundation, an organization dedicated to preserving those magnificent yet fragile birds on an international level.

On a previous bike tour through the area, I made a point of visiting the foundation. There were many interesting exhibits; however those earnest do-gooders lacked a sense of humor. When I jokingly asked if they knew where I could get a good grilled crane breast sandwich, they got all huffy. The cyclists I was with thought it was funny.

In the town of Dane, population 799, I read a historical sign. The town and the county were named after Nathan Dane and not the super-sized variety of dog. Nathan was a signer of the Declaration of Independence and helped create the Northwest Ordinance of 1787. He pushed the idea of prohibiting slavery in what was then considered the Northwest Territory. With his foresight, the future states of Ohio, Illinois, Michigan, and Wisconsin would be forever slave-free. For his bold action, a portion of Wisconsin decided to honor his name.

In Waunakee, the only Waunakee on the planet, I caught sight of Madison's state capitol building. As Elmer Fudd once said, "West and wewaxation at wast!" I weaved through the busy streets of Madison picking up offerings of beer, flowers and coffee for my hosts to be.

Big Al and Jean are a well-educated and dynamic couple whose intelligent and insightful conversations I yearned for. I needed a timeout from the ranting and ravings of my nightly bar-talk sessions.

Jean was a Madison city councilwoman for more than a decade: Her constituents loved her. When she wasn't dealing with the issues of Madison's eclectic political bent, she worked as a soil scientist for the state. She has a mind for detail and a memory to match. She's also very funny.

Big Al is a well-read librarian (aren't they all?) who was instrumental in turning me on to minor league baseball. For this I owe him for the many enjoyable hours I have spent in the simple pursuit of watching the game. He's also a walking and talking Google's-worth of knowledge with a sarcastic twist of humor. This dude knows his stuff.

Once safely in Madison, I had to rest my pitching arm for another stint in the pre-game lineup for the Madison Mallards. I had contacted Vern, the general manager, about my bicycle ride and baseball quest. Yes, I am shameless. He offered me the "pill." Who was I to turn him down?

The mound was busy as I was one of seven tossing out the first pitch. No matter – my pitch made it to the catcher without being stained by Mother Earth. I was beginning to get the hang of this pitching stuff. The ball was pink (or salmon for manly men) in honor of Breast Cancer Awareness Night at the "Duck Pond." That ball would eventually stand out in my ever-increasing collection.

The remainder of my rest-and-recovery days were spent eating, visiting friends, eating, quaffing beer, eating, and drinking coffee. I was energizing for the onslaught of the next few thousand miles (with detours) to Bar Harbor, Maine. I've spent time in worse ways, like working. As usual, Jean and Big Al were gracious hosts who didn't seem to mind me being me.

After two and a half days of sloth, it was time to get back into motion. All the pampering I was receiving from my hosts made me feel like I was beginning to put down roots. That would never do.

The morning of my departure from Mad-town was clammy and windless. Generous Jean and I went out for breakfast, where she presented me with a U.S. map. I was able to see my efforts in the big scale of things.

I left that wise couple and sought bike trails through the University of Wisconsin (Go Badgers!) with its scenic view of Lake Mendota, past State Street (bars, coffee houses, international restaurants, and T-shirt shops), a lap around the state capitol (smaller version of the U.S. Capitol) and continued on a northeast path out of town. Six miles later I was once again bisecting corn and soy fields along the alphabet-soup roads.

I was in low-energy mode and a bit sad to be leaving behind vibrant, quirky and friendly Madison. I decided to go short to Beaver Dam and make up the difference on the next day.

I bypassed the northern outskirts of Waterloo, where the Farm Technology Fair was in full swing. From what I gathered, regional farmers come from yonder and farther to size-up the latest advances in machinery to aid their ancient profession of growing food.

At one point, I wondered whether the police presence wasn't greater than the farmers. Personally, I never considered Captain Kangaroo's sidekick Mr. Green Jeans to be much of a threat. But then again, these days one can never be too careful, according to Fox News.

At Beaver Dam, I checked into another easy-on-my-wallet hotel. At least this one was clean enough not to require a "deodorizer machine." Later, I relaxed on the banks of Beaver Dam Lake and watched as fishermen and ducks floated about.

When dawn came I felt like a new me. The warmer temperatures, sunny skies and two heaping cups of "Kum & Go" gas station coffee didn't hurt either. There wasn't even a bovine's fart of a breeze in the air. Perfect!

It was typical Wisconsin riding as the roads switched between numbers and letters. In Waupun, I couldn't help but notice the large correctional institution. Did the sign displaying the town's population include the folks who would rather be somewhere else? No matter, it seemed to be an above-average town as far as the economic downturn was concerned. Maybe crime does pay!

Eventually I dropped into the Fox River Valley and home of Lake Winnebago. It's the largest lake that resides entirely in Wisconsin. Lake Winnebago is also famous for sturgeon spearing. In February, when the lake is one large ice rink, intrepid hunters try their luck at sticking the prehistoric fish. Ice houses containing well-stocked coolers keep the spear-chuckers happy, even if they don't haul in a big one. Local crews plow roads on the ice sheet. This is a Wisconsin big deal.

I plied my way through Oshkosh and its rampant display of shuttered businesses and homes for sale. Wisconsin had, unfortunately, just passed the 9 percent unemployment rate while I was traveling through. I thought I was dropping enough coin in the state to stimulate the local economy: guess not.

Just north of Oshkosh, I made a stop at Paynes Point bar and grill, a landmark roadhouse if there ever was one. There I picked up a sandwich for me and a 12-pack for my host for the evening, Bill Beaster. He is also known as the mayor of the GRABAAWR ride. If not for Bill, I would not have gleaned all those acquaintances in the Midwest. He's an old friend with whom I share many fond memories.

Bill is also a cancer survivor. In 1993, he felt something was not right down under, so he saw his doc for a checkup. After an exam and biopsy the results were not what he would have chosen to hear: Bill had testicular cancer. "Can you come in tomorrow so we can remove the cancerous testicle?" the doctor said.

A few months later, Cyclops (as his friends-for-life quickly nicknamed him) and I were riding a few hundred miles in a few days to get to Eagle River for the start of GRABAAWR. It was a tediously muggy and stifling day as we made our way through the farm-and-milk-cow countryside on a century jaunt. Bill looked wan and tortured.

We were very close to our destination when he stopped and said, "Screw it! I'm done!"

He pitched his bike to the side and sat down in a small pool of water in a roadside ditch.

"Come on, Bill! We're only five miles away. You can do it."

"Nope!" was all he said.

"I'll buy you a six-pack of Leinies!" I was not beyond bribery to motivate my buddy.

"OK. I'll come out and we'll finish this crappy ride." He said this with great resignation in his voice.

Once inside the confines of an air-conditioned hotel room, we opened the brews and quenched our thirst. Bill looked better after the first bottle. By the third, he was back to his normal, fun self. Beer was mother's milk for my German friend. This was the character I was about to visit and I was looking forward to it.

When I arrived, Bill was doing his usual thing of moving in 14 directions at the same time. He was busy readying his home for his wife's family reunion. Kay is Catholic; needless to say, it would be a large gathering. I assisted with the preparations when I could and kept out of the way when I couldn't.

By 7ish, Bill ran out of gas and it was beer-thirty time. I mostly listened as this former high school teacher espoused wisdom, strong opinions, facts, and rumors concerning old friends, world politics and other random subjects. Every now and then, I'd interject a comment. For the most part, I sat back, drank my beer and smiled. This was so much more enjoyable than drinking alone.

The next morning, I woke with the mandatory hangover that was the price for trying to keep pace with Bill. I said my goodbyes as he ramped up his energy level. Believe it or not, he does it caffeine-free. Fortunately, I had a short ride on my day's agenda. All that was impeding me was a cool, pissed–off wind, heaps of traffic and 28 miles to Appleton.

That Fox River city is famous for paper making, Harry Houdini (he claimed he was born there, but there are many non-believers) and being the home of the Wisconsin Timber-Rattlers baseball club. Which one do you think I was interested in?

As per my usual pre-game ritual, I sought and found the Stone Cellar brewpub. I took an outside seat and struck up a conversation with Mac. He was a chubby, 40-ish bloke who recently had a child with a half-his-age girlfriend. He sold Lexus automobiles for a living.

"How's business in the luxury-vehicle field these days?" I asked.

His answer surprised me: "If we can sell 60 each month, we're ahead of the game."

Apparently, paper-mill owners must still be making a good living. We exchanged ideas and stories as we drained off our brews and put the finishing touches on dinner. I headed off for baseball; he headed home to change diapers.

The Friday-night, family crowd at Fox Cities Stadium was there to watch fireworks in the air and hopefully on the field. I grabbed a beer and found my seat. Between the game, the intra-inning contests and watching the heavy traffic on nearby Highway 41, there was never a dull moment. The weather cooperated for a change and I wasn't scrambling for my jacket.

I lost momentum at the top of the ninth with the score tied. At 10 p.m., it was way past this cyclist's bedtime. I Googled the score the next day: Snakes smothered the Dayton Dragons 5-4 in 11 innings, for those who are keeping score.

I slept like a sleeping giant and woke to summer, but only for a moment en route to Green Bay. I followed the Fox River Valley north through the Hawaiian-sounding town of Kaukauna. In De Pere, which was named by an early French explorer, I gained a paved bike trail that led me right into downtown "Title Town."

Yes, I was in realm of Green Bay Packer mystique. But for me there would be no visions of Vince Lombardi; just another evening of four-corner baseball provided by the Green Bay Bullfrogs.

I spent a summer's night in Green Bay the previous year. This blue-collar town was visibly hurting then. In 2009, with the economy really spirally south, it appeared to be mortally wounded.

I wondered what Michigan with its 15 percent unemployment rate would be like. Chanting, "We're number one!" didn't seem appropriate for that dubious honor.

The Bullfrogs play in Joannes Stadium, which was built in 1929. The ballpark emulates Green Bay: basic, worn out and no frills. A quick-moving rain shower could not dampen the crowd's enthusiasm. But then again, die-hard Packer fans need to stay in shape in the off-season. I found a dry seat under an awning and watched a well-played match. After a run-saving tag out at home plate, the fans shouted an appreciative chorus of "Rib bit! Rib bit!" to honor their hometown amphibians. By the seventh inning stretch, this fan needed to stretch out on a bed.

I left Green Bay on another CCD (cool, clammy and dreary) morning. I had on a jacket to hold in some body heat as I passed stores in flip-a-coin mode as to whether they were "For Sale" or still in business. I skimmed along the empty streets until I found a café open eight miles from the city center. It was a fortunate find; the next café I saw was 35 miles farther on in Oconto. I would surely have been running on fumes by then.

Heading north along Lake Michigan, I heard the unmistakable snaps of gunfire. It seemed way too close for comfort. I felt puckered. Luckily, the hunters didn't confuse me for a bicycle-riding Bambi and I managed to keep out of their line of fire.

In Pensaukee, I learned the burg had once sustained the one and only commercial sawmill in the Michigan Territory (this included everything west of the Great Lakes to the Pacific Ocean) in 1827. That's a lot of forest for one mill.

I just missed a pool-forming cloudburst on Highway 41. The pavement was awash in leaping frogs and I did my best not to smear them. Kermit would have been pleased with my efforts. Rib-bit!

A few moments later, I entered Peshtigo. All seemed quiet and normal, but it was not so on Oct. 8, 1871. That was the date of the greatest loss of life by fire in U.S. history.

The Peshtigo fire claimed the lives of an estimated 1,200 to 2,400 people. The actual number was never ascertained due to the large area the fire consumed. More than 1.5 million acres of Northeastern Wisconsin and Upper Michigan were affected by the firestorm. A somber reminder can be seen in the Peshtigo Fire Cemetery, where the unidentifiable remains of hundreds of Peshtigo citizens are interned in a mass grave.

A sad irony: That date was the same as the Great Chicago Fire. Mrs. O'Leary's infamous cow created more headlines than this forgotten disaster north of the Windy City.

After the solemn history lesson, I sped over to Lee's Grocery to purchase a few gifts for retirees Pete and Maryanne, my willing hosts for the night. Once again, a Bill Beaster connection was coming through for me. There was no smoke or flames in sight as I made my way through a quiet, well-tended neighborhood to my benefactor's home.

Pete is a large man with a surprisingly impish grin. He had just returned from that rolling fraternity party in Iowa named RAGBRAI (Register's Great Annual Bike Ride Across Iowa.) He was a bit frayed from the ordeal and was in low-energy mode. No worries; so was I.

Maryanne prepared dinner while supplying a steady stream of banter and commentary. Pete and I sat back, enjoying the monologue and sipping our beverages. Here was a long-term couple who were quite sure of each other's roles. Their relationship is as efficient as a fit rider on a well-tuned bicycle. There were no bells, whistles or gimmicks. This was something to behold. I toddled off to bed after the banquet.

My perfect hosts fed me and caffeinated me up in the morning for my day's ride. After handshakes, hugs and a few photos, I set off with a sense of well-being. The appearance of a warming sun didn't hurt either. Unfortunately, it was only a cameo appearance. I returned onto busy Highway 41 and headed east over the Peshtigo River and past the now defunct paper mill.

A scant 10 miles later, I crossed over the Menomonee River and "Ya! Ya! You betcha!" I found myself in the Upper Peninsula of Michigan.

Moseying Through Michigan

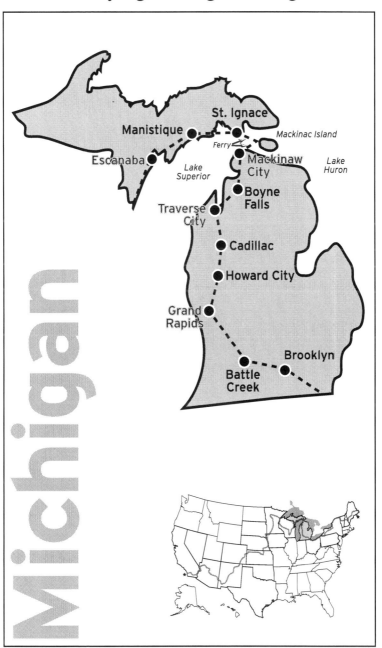

12. Moseying Through Michigan

"Engine Two, Engine One, Engine Six, Truck One, Squad Five, Battalion One, Westside ambulance, respond to a confirmed fire in a doublewide mobile home. We have had many calls on this. Informants say there is a woman trapped inside. Address is …"

It was another bleary-eyed wake-up call after midnight. A difference was this call was a short block from the station. We saw flames streaking high into the cave-black, moonless sky the second we opened the bay doors. This was not good. The report of a person trapped inside provided a jolt to wake up – NOW! We knew our first task would be an attempted rescue.

Our company officer, Randy, gave firefighter Brad and I a few calm directions in the short time it took us to roll up on scene.

"Jeff! Place a few hose lines at the front door. Brad! See if there's a way to gain entry for a rescue. I'll give a quick on-scene report and then help Brad."

A half-minute later I parked the engine past the flaming trailer, and we hit the ground running. While Randy reported what we had, what we were doing, and gave assignments to the incoming units, Brad looked for a way into the inferno. I placed hose lines at the front door while trying to block out the wailing cries of the victim. The horrible sound soon subsided.

Brad and a few bystanders pounded on a rear door to gain entry, but to no avail. The door would not yield. We found out later an overzealous landlord had used screws to lock the entrance for good.

Flames blew out of the shattered windows. This one was a cooker.

Randy donned an air pack. He and Brad tried to make entry into the trailer using an inch and three-quarter hose line. The nozzle was on full-bore but had no effect. It would take the flow of two more hose lines to knock down the fire. Brad found the victim and delivered her to the paramedics, but there was no save here. The 22-year-old woman succumbed to burns and smoke inhalation.

We wetted down the remaining flames and smokes and tried to minimize the destruction. The investigators moved in: The wood, metal and plastic that remained of the blackened heap was now a crime scene. The firefighters were spent physically and emotionally. For all of us returning to quarters that night, there would be no falling back to sleep.

For many nights after that call, sleep avoided me like a jilted girlfriend. I kept hearing the victim's anguished screams.

The Upper Peninsula of Michigan has always fascinated me. One does not require a degree in geography to fathom that this state-sized land mass is really attached to Wisconsin. I wrongly assumed those fun-loving cheeseheads were too busy eating bratwurst and drinking beer to notice pilfered property, but my assumption wasn't even close.

It all goes back to a disputed chunk of land named the "Toledo Strip." The established state of Ohio (1803) and the wannabe state of

Michigan were arguing about ownership of the strip and the city of Toledo. After the governor of Ohio dissed the territorial governor of Michigan, the militias of both jurisdictions were called to action. But the anticipated battle never occurred: The war parties could not find each other in the dense forest. All wars should be fought like this.

Eventually, the U.S. Congress said enough of this nonsense. Its response was short and brusque. Michigan, get over the Toledo Strip and you can have the Upper Peninsula in trade. We'll even throw in a few Yoopers (nickname for folks in the U.P.) for entertainment. That in a pasty shell is how the U.P. became part of Michigan. In 1837, statehood was granted, nine years before Wisconsin joined the fun.

I tumbled east along Highway 35, passing a multitude of second homes with names such as Fisherman's Haven, Tiki Bar, Paradise Found and of course, Margaritaville. Many had "For Sale" signs stuck to the mailboxes. Vacation getaway homes might have been too extravagant in Michigan's dismal economy.

Convoys of logging trucks paraded by bearing potential Sunday N.Y. Times to the pulp mills. I managed to keep out of their way.

For the most part, the view of Lake Michigan was obscured by the bulk of spruce, hemlock, pine, and hardwoods adjacent to the roadway. Once in a while a county park would provide a tease of a look-see.

Upon entering Delta County, I arrived in the Eastern Time Zone. I had lost three hours of time since departing from San Diego. No wonder it took me so long to get anywhere.

After 63 miles of wind-driven effort, I arrived in the Spanish-sounding city of Escanaba. The name is actually a Native American derivative that translates to "red buck" or "eat rock." Whichever you prefer, this community happens to be the second most populated city (13,000) in the U.P. Obviously, population control in the U.P. is not a hot political topic.

It's a port town complete with a lighthouse. Freighters pick up iron ore here for transport east to Chicago and northern Indiana. The lumber mill is the largest employer.

Escanaba (the river, at least) is also famous as being mentioned in Henry Wadsworth Longfellow's epic poem, "The Song of Hiawatha." There's an overabundance of places named for this legendary Ojibwa Indian, including the nearby national forest, an adjacent town of 1,300, the Hiawatha Trail, the Hiawatha Golf Course and my motel, which on its sign proclaimed, "Love is the answer to all of your questions. Free Wi-Fi."

I had an uneventful evening and got plenty of shut-eye. I moved east on quiet side roads on a shockingly sunny morning. I placed a wet finger into the air. Yes! Tailwind! With a pot of strong coffee in me and a wonderful push from behind, I felt invincible. No wonder Tour de France rules limit racers to two cups of java. It is a drug.

Later, I rejoined my old buddy Highway 2. It shoots straight east through Hiawatha National Forest void of any communities but has plenty of runty trees. No surprise there with the short growing season and boggy soils.

Near Thompson, I found a sign on the lake-view side of the road carrying a sad history lesson. Off the nearby shore, the Rouse Simmons – the Christmas Tree ship – sank in 1912.

The schooner was bound for Chicago with a load of Christmas trees. Apparently, skipper Herman Schuenemann ignored a sudden drop in barometric pressure and an increase in wind speed. According to the historical account, even the rats left the ship. But the crew and captain never made it. All 16 hands went down with the ship. Surely not a Merry Christmas for the bereaved families.

I spent the night in Manistique. The name is a French corruption of what the Ojibwa called the nearby "River of the big bay." It's a groovy little town with a two-mile boardwalk hugging Lake Michigan. The stroll terminates at the East Breakwater Lighthouse. Despite its blood red color, the lighthouse provides a reassuring beacon to passing ships. Unfortunately, there are no lighthouse keepers with whom to share a cup of coffee or conversation. The light has been on autopilot since 1968.

I watched seagulls glide above the dancing whitecaps. It was an ocean-like scene on the sixth largest freshwater lake in the world. Jean Nicolet was the first white guy to see the lake in 1634. He was somewhat misguided as he was looking for a route to China. One would think he noticed the Winnebago Indians around Green Bay didn't look Chinese.

That's OK; Columbus thought the natives of the New World were from Asia. Americans forgave him for his mistake and created a bank holiday in his honor. What a country!

After another outstanding night of rest, I decided to go long (91 miles) to St. Ignace. During the first half of my day's ride, Highway 2 played keep away from the lake. One highlight was a hand-scrawled sign. It was as simple as its poor spelling: "For Sale!

Retirees, sideliners, bissness oportny. As one unit." Behind the advertisement was a trash heap of chairs, toilets, blue tarps, and one forlorn camper. The seller didn't believe in sprucing up the joint for the big sale. It made me want to write a check out on the spot – NOT!

The scenery improved quickly heading east toward Naubinway, where the road and the lake become one. At Pointe Aux Chenes, sand dunes and the swells came into sight. Once again, I had to pinch myself to believe I wasn't already in Maine along the Atlantic Ocean. Intrepid Midwesterners swam in the icy waters. The only thing missing was the scent of salt water.

A few miles short of St. Ignace, I pulled off the road to take a good gander at the third longest suspension bridge in the world. The Mackinac Bridge is a five-mile engineering marvel that spans the Straits of Mackinac. It connects the Upper Peninsula with mainland Michigan. It replaced an antiquated ferry system in 1957 and is now part of Interstate 75.

Crossing the span on a bicycle is taboo, and for good reason. In 1989, a Yugo plunged over the side and into the drink. The cause of the wreck was excessive cross winds (Mother Nature) and excessive speed (human error.) For me, the risk wasn't worth it.

I called the epic ride done when I pulled into St. Ignace, which sits on the banks of Lake Huron. Another day, another Great Lake: A fella could get used to this.

St. Ignace happens to be one of the oldest towns in the United States. It was founded by French Jesuits way back in 1671. It stayed French until the British wrestled it away and finally became an

198

American possession after the Revolutionary War. As of this writing, it is still part of the United States.

At one time it was a fur-trading center. Then fishing took over. Presently, tourism seems to be the main gig.

I immediately felt a bond with the place while watching ferries, cabin cruisers and sailboats ply the straits. A lovely red-and-white lighthouse watched over things. Along the shoreline, a mink scuttled among the pebbles.

You're a Baby Boomer if you can remember dad proudly presenting your mom with a coat made up of these critters as an anniversary gift. My Mom was practically gushing when she received hers. Today, PETA (People for the Ethical Treatment of Animals) would have a strong opinion on that type of gift giving. The specimen I saw made me a fine set of mittens. (Only kidding.)

Toward sunset, I took libations and a fish fry at the "Marina Bar and Grill." The bar stools faced out, overlooking the bay. It was a nice change from the typical Midwestern tavern where dead animals glare down while you catch a buzz. The burly, tattooed bartender noticed my smile as I admired the placid scene.

"About 30 years ago, the bar faced away from the bay. I guess they didn't care much for views in those days," he said with a smirk.

Sitting next to me at the bar were Hank and his wife, Kate, up from Detroit on a mini-vacation.

"We paid for our son's law school and never took a day off in seven years. We hope that pays off for all in the long run," Hank said.

This hard-working couple told me about their visit to nearby Mackinac Island. They made a confession: "We rented bicycles over there, rode out one mile and said, 'Screw this!'"

I told them they would have to do better than that in order to join me the rest of the way to Maine. They got a chuckle out of that as they wished me a sincere "good luck!"

I slept like crap. (Too tired? Too much brew? Both?) Somehow, I managed to catch the 9:30 a.m. ferry to Mackinac Island. I was in need of a mellow, relaxed and no-sweat day of cycling. I had a feeling Mackinac would be just the ticket.

The island lies strategically on Lake Huron at the eastern edge of the Straits of Mackinac. Our fledgling nation fought the British for sole possession of this military plum and won. Once again, fur and fish ruled the roost until the rich folks discovered the place and built mansions on its bluffs. The entire island is a National Historical Landmark, and rightfully so.

After rolling off the ferry, I experienced a feeling of peace and tranquility immediately. No cars! Forward motion is limited to pedestrians, bicycles and horse-power. Essential goods and services move about by man-hauled carts or horse-drawn drays. It's this step backward that draws tourists to this limestone jewel.

Visitors who had not been on a bicycle for 25 years were out pedaling around the eight-mile rim road. Multiple generations of families were strung out along slow-moving pace lines. It was a grand scene and woke me from my stupor.

While I was out and about doing a lap, many fellow riders asked me about my loaded steed. My answer? "Do you think I packed too much for an eight-mile ride?"

After seeing some of the sights of the island, I was interviewed by Kerri from the Town Crier, the local newspaper. It must have been a slow news day on Paradise Island. After my 15 minutes of fame, the weather became noticeably cooler with a dose of drizzle. Since I had not won the Powerball lottery (hotels on Mackinac Island are pricey), I chose to return to the mainland of Michigan and overnight in Mackinac City. It was a bumpy ferry ride across the straits.

While St. Ignace has an easygoing, laid-back feel about it, Mackinac City is anything but that. According to AAA (American Automobile Association) stats, Mackinac City is the most popular tourist destination in Michigan. Large families wandered up and down the Main Street poking into fudge, T-shirt and ice cream shops. Most of the buildings were new and built in function-over-form mode. Mackinac City is really a village whose population increases exponentially in the short summer tourist season. The place does have a few draws: the Mackinac Bridge, another lighthouse, Mackinac Island ferries, and a decommissioned ice breaker. With the unseasonably cool weather, I could almost envision ice bergs forming along the straits.

I escaped from the marauding families into a quiet pub, opting for a short night out to save my energy for a long meander to Boyne Falls and friends.

I hit the road early. The hordes were asleep and traffic was nil. No complaints there. I swept past the still waters of Lake Michigan and beaches devoid of anything but sand. A small detour to be in Bliss – as in Bliss, Mich., not the feel-good state of mind – seemed in order. It would have been a wonderful place to overnight, as in "I slept in Bliss!" But it was not meant to be. There were no accommodations there, anyway. My ex-girlfriends were safe: I usually slept in bliss with them.

Honestly, the naming of the town had nothing to do with a feeling of well-being. The place was named in honor of a post Civil War governor of Michigan. That's a name that surely would draw a lot of votes. Who would vote against Bliss?

I came across Michigan Road 119, which is nicknamed the Tunnel of Trees Heritage Road. It's a lane-and-a-half conveyance with no center line or anyone in a rush to get anywhere. The route pivots, takes dips and undulates through an abundance of hardwoods and ferns. I stopped for a respite and heard nothing but the melodic sounds of songbirds performing. Perfect!

I was in the "zone" when another cyclist snuck up on me and asked, "Where are you heading?"

I gave him the Reader's Digest version of my journey and he informed me that he was a Harbor Springs psychologist. That's when the questions came hot and heavy.

"So why are you doing this, really?"

"You would have me committed if you knew the truth!" My answer was closer to reality than my laugh would reveal to him.

The shrink became my tour guide as we entered Harbor Springs, another former lumber-and-fishing town that's now an enclave for the fabulously wealthy of the Midwest. I kidded the doc by asking him which lakeside mansion was his. He confided in me that many of his patients reside in those estates. Sad to think that even those with no monetary issues could be mental, too.

He soon sped off to soothe another tortured soul. He was running late and the affluent don't like to be kept waiting.

I turned inland away from the Great Lake and the rich folks. With the help of a few AAA maps, I found back roads running toward Boyne Falls. In winter, skiers and boarders descend upon the nearby slopes of the Boyne Mountain Resort. From my vantage point on Highway 131, I detected a shaved hillside to the right. It wasn't a clear-cut lumber operation; it was a Midwest version of a ski mountain, all 500 vertical feet of it. I could see why the ski slopes of Colorado are stacked with Midwesterners.

My hostess, Cathy, was waiting for me at the resort lodge. I had met Cathy and her spousal unit, Mark, during the Bicycle Tour of Colorado in the summer of 2007. They are an upbeat and positive couple, despite all the chaos in the world, and I feel fortunate to know them.

Cathy led me uphill to her home. I was surprised in a good way when I saw her pad, which looked like a smaller version of the famous Yellowstone Lodge. This was one large log home tastefully done on the inside and out. Mark is a commercial real estate contractor and developer; he might have had something to do with the house. He proudly announced it was built with 100 percent union labor. Whoever constructed it left behind a work of art.

That evening I slept well in the dark, cool and quiet basement. When I journeyed upstairs for coffee and breakfast, I noticed the slick gray skies holding the for-sure promise of moisture and wind. I looked at my kind hosts and asked for a day of bicycle reprieve from the elements. They graciously granted me an extended stay.

We had a leisurely morning of drinking coffee, catching up on each other's lives and writing in my journal. Cathy had been one busy woman in her retirement, always coming or going on some outdoor adventure. One trait I share with her is a reluctance to sit still for very long periods. That day was no exception.

The weather improved marginally, so we went for a three-mile hike, including Mark. He's a punster and an easygoing Midwesterner with a flair for business and getting things done. They appeared to be a yin-and-yang couple, with each one bringing strong points to their relationship.

When the lashing rains returned, we retreated to the security of a Mexican restaurant in Boyne City. The chips, salsa, margaritas, and burritos went down as well as our threads of conversation. The rest of the day was spent along these lines.

The next chilly morning, Cathy and Mark volunteered to lead me out for the first 30 miles of riding to Blaire. Cathy summed up the weather brilliantly: "It's a beautiful day … for October!" They donned hats, gloves, vests and arm warmers. I pretty much wore my whole wardrobe. I had to ask if this had been a "normal" summer of weather. Cathy thought for a nanosecond: "Hell no! Usually it's hot, steamy and hardly any wind. This summer we've only noticed the few days when the wind wasn't howling."

I was happy to hear the meteorological events I had witnessed weren't just products of my vivid imagination. Then, as if on cue, the headwind machine started up again. "Welcome to my world!" I shouted above the gusts.

They guided me along highly scenic and serene Sunday morning roads to Blaire. At a coffeehouse, we warmed up with drinks, muffins and quiches before parting ways. I scored a cuddly hug from Cathy and a manly handshake from Mark. They pointed me in the right direction and once again I was alone.

Away I went up a hill and into the chilling wind. At Rapid City, I enquired about directions to Traverse City. Here was the answer: "If you see a strip joint, you have gone too far." I had never received directions quite like that before.

The traffic was so annoying I didn't notice the "peeler" bar. Where did all these vacationers come from in this recession? With all the commotion around me, I was soon missing the mellowness of the Upper Peninsula. On the outskirts of Traverse City I scored a room in an overpriced Econo Lodge motel. It had taken me eight hours of steady effort to cover 75 miles.

I had a whole hour to shower, eat dinner and drink a few beers before the Traverse City Beach Bums took on the Florence (Kentucky) Freedom. It only took one email to the team's co-owner to be set up with a free ticket. I was beginning to think that maybe I should email bankers for free samples. I was on a roll.

Wuefel Stadium, which is named after that nice woman who gave me a ticket, looks like a U-shaped cluster of townhomes when viewed from the front. My mistake: Those were just the backsides of luxury boxes. Apparently, plenty of money built this impressive park and a Great Lake's worth of cash keeps it going. I ventured to the "will call" box to procure my freebie. The kind young woman said, "You have a choice of tickets. Where would you like to sit?"

"How about somewhere warm, sunny and away from the wind?" I innocently replied.

I landed in the ninth row behind the dugout. The seat came complete with sunrays and more importantly, no freaking wind. Once again, baseball would provide emotional and physical succor to my tired body and soul.

Despite many errors and the sight of seeing not one but two batters fling their bats into the stands (fortunately, no spectators were injured), it was the highlight of my long day. The Bums showed the Freedom who ruled that Sunday evening with a 9-5 drubbing. For me, it was lights out soon after the final out.

The sound of thunder and full-on rain woke me in the morning. I managed to procrastinate until there was a break in the weather. It was 9-ish when I turned south into a drizzle and headwind. By the time I arrived in Mesick for a second breakfast, it had been more than 120 minutes and a mere 21 miles of motion. It was time for a decision: If I continued down this path of futility, the pummeling would continue for way too long. Screw it! I decided to cut my angst and hobble to Cadillac (18 miles farther) instead.

The run to Lake Mitchell and Lake Cadillac was relatively downhill. Manistee National Forest provided the trees, which seemed to act as windbreaks. Once again, I had to agree with the poet Joyce Kilmer, "I think that I will never see, a poem lovely as a tree."

Cadillac is a city of 10,000 residents spread out between two lakes. One cool factoid: The heavy metal band Kiss played at the 1975 homecoming held at Cadillac High School. Rock on!

A canal connects the two lakes, making it a hit among the fishermen. In the past, logging with the aid of the Shay's locomotive to ascend the steep grades supported the local economy until the resource became harder to come by. The forests were depleted by overzealous ax-men. Now tourism and manufacturing keep the city afloat.

I rented a room in a one-star motel with a five-star view of Lake Mitchell. Outside my dingy domicile were barbeques, coolers, lawn chairs, and clunker cars telling me my neighbors weren't just overnight guests. When I eventually win the Powerball lottery, I plan to continue bicycle touring; I'll sleep in a lot better motels, though.

Evidently, I slept through a night of extreme weather. In the morning I waded the bike through the parking lot between puddles large enough to maintain schools of carp. I found a dirt path between the two lakes and I plunged in.

This was the humble beginning of the White Pine Trail State Park, a 92-mile route that was once the right of way for the Grand Rapids and Indiana Railroad. In 1994, the state of Michigan pulled up the tracks and declared it a state park. The trail meandered from Cadillac to Comstock Park. The end point happened to be a baseball stadium. Lucky me!

At first the trail lured me in with a surface of crushed gravel and sand. The gritty blend quickly coated my gears and chain: challenging but doable. Then it morphed into a short-grass prairie, where a lawn mower would have been useful. I felt rewarded for my extra efforts by the silence and greenery. I chased the occasional whitetail deer off the trail as deer flies chased me.

The trail's namesake tree had apparently succumbed to Paul Bunyan and company. Now a diverse hardwood forest stood adjacent to the trail. Every few miles stood a majestic white pine that escaped the logger's ax. A smooth-as-glass asphalt surface greeted me in Reed City and I saw other humans for the first time along the route. After Big Rapids, the trail retreated back to grit and gravel. I said enough already.

I entered Old Highway 131 near Stanwood. This turned out to be a great decision as I inadvertently discovered a part of Michigan's Amish country. The giveaway was the horse-and-buggy signs along the road advising motorists of the unusual road hazard.

I passed fields where hay was stacked in handmade "shocks" to cure. An Amish teenager with a 5 o'clock shadow of a beard wearing a wide-brimmed hat walked by me carrying a sickle. In the opposite direction, a horse-and-buggy carrying a bonneted grandma clip-clopped by. Signs sprouted up along the roadside announcing, "Fresh brown eggs and vegetables for sale. No sales on Sunday!" All the properties had a delightfully lush and manicured appearance. This was a different type of eye-candy that appealed to me. By the time I got to Morley, the simple-living Amish were gone, replaced once again by the 21st century.

I took a room in the appropriately named "Tour-Inn" motel in Howard City. Despite being immaculate and inexpensive, I was the sole guest. I surmised Howard City might be off the radar of summer vacationers. Their loss.

When it was time for dinner, I wandered a quarter of a mile downtown to the Latitudes bar and grill. A wave of cigarette fumes struck me like a tsunami as I entered. I was tempted to drop to my knees and "crawl low in smoke" as I did in bygone days.

After being seated at a small table, I ordered a beer, a meal and a bottle of oxygen (only joking.) I entertained myself by watching the Detroit Lions play ball on the big screen TV.

I was minding my own business when Matt halted in front of me while en route to the men's room and introduced himself. "What tribe are you from?" he said as he extended his hand for a shake.

Not the usual, "Hi! How's it hanging?"

He wore a "Native American" ball cap with a mourning dove feather tucked in the side.

"Well, I guess I am from the tribe of Abraham," I said.

He thought for a second, wavered a bit and replied, "Never heard of them. Where do you live?"

"Colorado!"

"Is that by Kansas or Wyoming?"

"Yep! You are in the ballpark."

Finally his urge to go overcame his desire for answers. When he returned to his bar stool, I overheard him asking a neighbor, "What tribe are you from?" I think Matt sees Native Americans in everyone.

After draining my beer and finishing my sandwich, I decided to give my lungs a break and left. Fresh air never felt so good as I pushed open the front door.

Fall was in the air when I woke the next morning, but at least it was a sunny day. I made it as far as Sand Lake before my tank hit empty. At the Stage Stop café I made small talk with George.

"Well, kiddo! I just retired after serving in the military for a long time," he said. "Wish I had the energy to do what you are doing. I keep busy doing projects around my place." He paused to collect his thoughts and said, "With the long winters, I sometimes run out of projects. I don't like that. Now I'm waiting for a few friends to show. I'm in a traveling breakfast club. We meet within a 30-mile radius of Sand Lake."

A few moments later, George's companions limped in with the aid of three canes and one walker. They were four elderly matrons. I bent an ear to their breakfast banter. Let's just say George turned out to be an equal opportunity flirter.

I returned to a paved White Pine Trail to complete the ride to Comstock Park. Unlike the roughed up 4x4 section I had traversed, this smoothie contained riders. It was an entertaining cross section of humanity on bikes: wavering kids, worrisome moms, proud dads showing Junior how it's done, all-women gangs jabbering away, and my favorite, a bunch of gents who could have stepped out of a "Flomax" commercial.

In Rockford (home of Wolverine boots), it was time for a pick-me-up latte. The town is an upscale bedroom community of Grand Rapids. While listening to the Rogue River gurgle by, I noticed well-coifed women darting in and out of boutique shops. If Michigan was in an economic thither, one would never have known from Rockford. That boot company must be kicking butt!

It was a pleasant ride to Orchard Park, where I planned to meet Big Dick from Detroit. No, he's not a porn star; he is more than a foot taller than me. He and I would be taking in the Grand Rapids Whitecaps vs. Dayton Dragons contest at Fifth Third Field.

I met Dick on the Bike South 2000 tour. The ride was advertised as a once-per-millennium event. The tour took in six southern states in five weeks and 2,000 miles. The ride directors were hoping to sign up 2,000 interested riders, but the true number was closer to 250. Big Dick and I were among them.

In 2000, Dick had recently retired from a career in journalism. He was a happy-go-lucky, stooped-shouldered guy with a wisp of a white ponytail. He quickly became a member of our exclusive Happy Hour group. His observations about life, politics and general knowledge were insightful and entertaining, a rare gift.

Almost 10 years later and age 76, Big Dick was a bit more bent over and a half-step slower. The good news; his happy-go-lucky disposition had not budged one iota. I could see that the old newspaper man still had a keen "eye" for a good story. It was great to see this lanky senior citizen once again.

When he arrived at the Swan Hotel, I helped him unpack gear from his dependable Subaru. Soon after we lovingly placed my steed in the back. We were en route to the ballpark. I had an appointment to ride around the outfield and heave the first pitch – again.

I notified Mickey Graham, director of marketing and media, about my baseball lust via an email. I was hoping to score a few freebies. He bettered the deal by providing me with tickets and a first pitch. All I had to do was provide pedal power for my entry. This time I was hoping a N.Y. Yankees scout would be on hand to notice me. Dream on!

I entered the ballpark through a back gate as a PA announcer intoned a spiel about my ride. He even pronounced my name right! I worked my way around the warning track, parked my bike near the dugout and jogged to the mound. This time my pitch was a high and wide. It was an off-speed pitch with little zing. Hey, even Sandy Koufax threw a ball every now and then. With a brand new baseball for my collection, I completed my lap around the outfield. I might have hammed it a bit with my queen's wave to the fans.

With another 15 seconds of fame over, I joined Dick in the ninth row behind home plate. I'm not sure who enjoyed this outing more; the Whitecap pitcher who managed eight innings of shut-out ball, Dick or me. Let's just call it a draw.

After a groggy night's rest but fortified on cheapo hotel coffee, I had to hightail it to Battle Creek to catch another game. I said a quick goodbye to Dick as he watched me leave the parking lot. No worries: Our time apart would be short. Our plan was to meet at a Toledo Mud Hens game.

I departed feeling an unfamiliar sensation. For the first time in weeks, it felt like summer. There was not even a hint of chill that balmy morning. Who needs sleep when one is caressed by summer's soothing temperatures?

It took some time to negotiate beyond the eastern outskirts of Grand Rapids. (Gerald Ford, our countries 38th president was a 12-term congressman from there.) At mile 15, two strange events occurred. One, the sun seemed to be rising in the west and I was supposed to be headed east. Two, when I glanced at my AAA map, I had barely moved half an inch from Grand Rapids. Sadly, there were many inches separating me from Battle Creek. I knew I was in for a long day.

I decided to seek knowledgeable directions for a more direct route. I spotted a local who might know. He was doing chores in the mid-morning sun outside his farmhouse.

"Sir! I'm looking for 5 Mile Road that might take me to Lincoln Road. Are you familiar with those roads?"

His answer was not the one I wished to hear: "Yep! You turned too soon. You need to go back one mile. Where are you heading?"

"Battle Creek."

A woman's voice sprang out from the inside of the house: "He can ride to Ada, and then take the Buttrick Road to …"

The man rolled his eyes and turned his back to me. Laura bounded out of the home. "Wow! I always wanted to do a cross-country ride," she said. "Come on in for breakfast. We are about to eat." Her hubby Darryl really rolled his eyes then.

"I don't know about breakfast. I don't think your husband is keen for my company."

"Don't mind him. He doesn't ride bikes."

That's what it took for me to be sitting in a 100-year-old farmhouse with a plate of food in front of me. I made a mental sticky-note to ask strangers for directions more often.

When we were done with the meal, the longtime married couple escorted me back to my bike. Darryl had me figured out in a short time: "His bike is so heavy because he's carrying a case of beer in there."

Am I that transparent?

We shot a few photos, exchanged email addresses and a highlight of that day came to an end. I caught a glancing hug from Laura. That was a cue for Darryl to roll his eyes once again.

I followed Laura's directions to Ada, which happens to be the site of Amway's world headquarters. I rode by the main entryway, which displayed a parade of flags from around the globe fluttering in the slight breeze. For a moment, I had a strange desire to invite 2,500 of my closest friends to watch a slide show on a wonderful life-changing business opportunity. But by the time I reached the outskirts of cozy Ada, I had nixed the idea. It wasn't a stressful thing for me or my friends to pick up a few bars of soap at Target.

The rest of the day's ride was mellow, complete with tailwinds, bogs, farms and forest to grab my attention. The miles piled up before I saw a sign for Battle Creek, aka Cereal City.

The city got its nickname from being the home of two cold cereal giants: Post and Kellogg. I half expected the streets to be crunchy and paved with Special K and Raisin Bran. A local informed me that at one time a bitter rivalry between the two employers was quite prevalent. Post workers wouldn't associate with Kellogg workers and vice versa. After all, the story goes, "You wouldn't want your sister to marry one."

Riding through town, I sensed an armistice in the Cereal Civil War. Both sides had a larger and winner-take-all nemesis: The real cereal killer around these parts was the recession. Businesses were shuttered in crumbling neighborhoods. Doorways and windows were boarded up with cut-to-fit plywood slabs. Where were all the people?

The downtown was struggling to keep its big-city feel alive. Beautifully paved bike and pedestrian trails ran along the Battle Creek River, but there was an absence of citizens to enjoy them. Even the Kellogg Museum was closed.

Kellogg's presence is still quite apparent. There is a Kellogg Community College, Kellogg Arena, Kellogg Auditorium, and Kellogg Foundation based within the confines of this once thriving city.

After a clean up and a change of clothes, I had time to enjoy Happy Hour and dinner at the Arcadia Brew Pub. After drinking a few delectable rye beers, I realized the cereal companies weren't the only ones around these parts who understood grains.

I asked the bartender about Cereal City. He answered between pours: "It's a nice place to live, despite the economic downturn. On Tuesdays, Kellogg makes Fruit Loops and the whole area reeks of it."

With that I rode upstream along the bike path to the very utilitarian C.O. Brown Stadium to watch a Battle Creek Bombers vs. Green Bay Bullfrogs match up. A huge (by Battle Creek standards) crowd was on hand to catch the final home game of the season. I'm sure free tickets and two-for-one beers had nothing to do with the influx of people. I made it to the seventh inning with the score tied 2-2 before I decided to call it. I'll admit it; I was beat. Next time, I'll eat my Wheaties.

On another chilly, wear-a-jacket morning, I headed out of Battle Creek on Michigan Avenue to Marshall. My route was once part of U.S. Route 12, a main thruway connecting Detroit to Chicago. It was replaced by Interstate 94 in 1962.

Marshall is a town easy to fall in love with. In 1830, early settlers had a bout of wishful thinking and expected the town to be named the state capital of Michigan. This hopeful attitude brought in the well-to-do, who built fine homes, churches, and government buildings. The state capital dream never materialized; Lansing scored that honor. Many of the risk-taking rich folks moved 46 miles north to Lansing. Lucky for Marshall, they left their buildings behind.

The National Register of Historic Places describes the town as a "virtual textbook of 19th century architecture." Marshall has one of our nation's largest National Historic Landmark Districts with a whopping 850 buildings included.

It's also a town with a history of social conscience. An "Underground Railroad" connection for slaves attempting to escape southern masters went through Marshall. The kindness of strangers was surely proven in the Crosswhite Incident of 1846.

Adam Crosswhite and his family were on the lam and nearly captured by Kentucky slave chasers in Marshall. The town's leading citizens decided to give those honkies a taste of their own medicine and arrested them. The Crosswhites completed their journey to Canada peacefully under the guidance of Marshall's townsfolk. Rescuers and rescued are buried within a few hundred feet of each other in the local cemetery.

I was so intrigued by the town's overall niceness, I stopped at the visitor center to learn more. Free-smiling Karen told me about the failed bid to become state capital and a few other factoids. "If you like it now, come back around Christmas. It's like a Norman Rockwell painting. Of course, you wouldn't want to arrive on a bicycle then."

Sound advice.

Continuing east, I came across Albion in time for second breakfast. The distance between the towns was only 11 miles, but the look of prosperity was worlds apart. At Alice's Restaurant (I'm pretty certain this is not the same one made famous by Arlo Guthrie), I spoke to Ralph as he dove into his burger and fries.

"This town's hurting," he said. "The foundry closed. They made farm implement and car parts. Lots of jobs were lost. People now are just trying to get by."

I noticed that the menu prices reflected this downturn. Compared to other towns in more upscale areas, Alice was practically serving her food for free.

On the outskirts of town, I veered off Michigan Avenue and joined Albion Road. The road builders must have been influenced by America's father of landscape architecture, Frederick Law Olmsted. The route bisected a forest of ash, oaks and maples with their branches intertwining in the middle. All was still and serene in there.

At Conway, a local advised me to take the Falling Waters Trail. It turned out to be another rail-to-trail effort, which seems so prevalent in the Midwest. I met Ray coming up from the opposite direction. He wore old-fashioned athletic shorts, a slight paunch and a big grin.

"I bought this mountain bike with full suspension. I know it's more bike than I'll ever need. I like the comfortable ride it gives me with my fused back. With this disability, I spend lots of my time riding up and down this trail."

I gave him an "atta Ray!" for still riding.

He gave my loaded rig the once over and remarked, "Wish I would have gone cross-country when I had a better body."

I suggested that maybe his wife could provide the SAG (support and gear) for a cross-country attempt.

"Nope! I don't think she loves me that much!"

We shook hands before parting ways as Ray continued down that trail for the umpteenth time.

I followed a general southeast direction to Brooklyn, (not New York) Mich. I was fortunate to have arrived when I did. A few days later and I would have been rubbing elbows and other parts with 100,000 rabid NASCAR fans. The nearby Michigan International Speedway was preparing for the onslaught. I would not been able to score a hotel room within 30 miles of Brooklyn. I looked at it this way: I saved the speed junkies a dose of boredom by not having to see me ride at 10 mph instead of 200 mph. However, I would have saved them the cost of a set of earplugs.

I turned in early for some catch-up beauty rest and woke to wet stuff on the ground and in the air. I dawdled until 9:30 a.m. and had to make a move. After all, I had a date with Big Dick and the Toledo Mud Hens.

Soon my bike shirts and shoes were squishy wet. By the time I arrived in Ottawa Lakes, I was in need of a hydration-and-rid-myself-of-hydration break. The fire station's bay doors were open, so I went in seeking shelter from the storm.

The guys had just completed washing the fire engines. Now the crew was gathered around Captain Gary. I inadvertently interrupted a lesson plan when I made entry. No one seemed upset as Gary asked me in true fire department hospitality, "Care for a cup of coffee?"

"Sure!" as I heard the drumming of a cloudburst on the station's roof.

I followed Gary upstairs, where he poured me a cup. While we drank our java he gave me the low-down on the fire department.

"The speedway's race officials contract with our department to provide emergency services for the event. They pretty much pay for our total annual budget."

Now I understood why this volunteer fire department in a town of 1,000 had such top-of-the-line equipment. They could afford it!

Gary continued: "We set up an Incident Command camper in the woods and wait for all the craziness to happen. We are very busy in that short time span."

I shook my head knowingly.

The other hat that Gary wore was a quality-control officer at the nearby Ford Motor Co. plant. "Lately, there's been some overtime at the plant. Maybe things are beginning to turn around. We make a good product. If an owner takes care of general maintenance, a Ford engine will turn over 300,000 miles."

Gary took pride in the work he performed in his community and beyond. It made me happy to know there are still Americans like him out there.

The rain let up as I drained my coffee. I thanked Gary for the hot beverage and said, "Be safe out there!" Once again, I never mentioned to these volunteers what I did before I rode bicycles for long distances.

I took another break at the halfway point in Blissfield. Beckey's Kountry Kitchen beckoned me through the rain-sopped streets.

An energetic waitress took my order as she asked me the four standard questions: "Where are you from? Where did you start? Where are you going? How many flats have you had?"

While I feasted on another super-sized Midwest breakfast, a large, friendly man ambled over. "Why are you doing your ride?"

"Because I can! I'm also retired and have plenty of time on my hands."

"Are you riding for some charitable cause?" he asked.

"Well, if someone wants to donate to the Lance Armstrong Foundation, I can set them up with a link to my page. I would be happy to email the donor photos and thoughts along my way. I would also take the time to give them a sincere thank you!" All of this was true.

"Mind if I take your photo and ask you a few questions for the local newspaper?"

"Sure!" The paparazzi always seem to find me!

I discovered that Randy was the owner of Beckey's. "Where's Beckey?" I asked.

"That's my last name," Randy admitted.

"Oh! I thought that maybe you had a sex change operation," I quipped. Good thing he had a sense of humor. He was a big man.

Randy took a few photos with his iPhone as he asked the four questions. I figured he was just trying to get his facts straight. Outside, I fidgeted with my bike while I answered a few more questions. I was preparing for the worst: everything in plastic bags.

"That will do! I'll post it on YouTube."

"What? I didn't know I was being filmed!"

"Yep! An iPhone can do that too!"

What do I know about technology? I just learned the wonders of "cut and paste" on my laptop. Somewhere out there on YouTube is 30 seconds of me giving disdainful glances at the drizzle. I might have smiled twice during the interview.

I was dodging puddles on a well-groomed shoulder when I noticed the "Welcome to Sylvania" sign. Immediately the road surface became pot-holed, with a narrow lane and just plain scary. I had entered Ohio and the once hotly contested "Toledo Strip."

Oh My! In Ohio

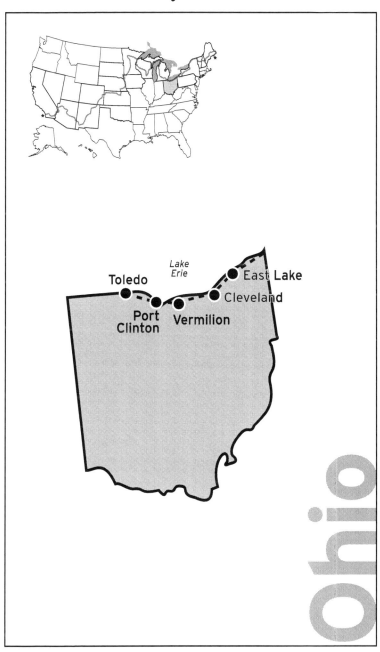

13. Oh My in Ohio

"Engine Two, Westside ambulance! Respond to an apparent shotgun suicide at … The police have also been dispatched to secure the scene."

I had been asleep for a few hours when the call came in. Shotgun suicides evoke the worst of pre-on-scene, gut-wrenching emotions. Many emergency service workers just hope: Please, not a head shot.

The cops were on scene as we marched in to confirm, "Yeah, the guy is dead."

The self-made victim performed the final deed standing up. It was an abdomen shot. Cloth from his blown out shirt was splattered on a basement wall, and the victim was resting in a pool of his own blood. A pet cat was lapping away at its former master's essence.

I've never been a fan of felines. After this call, I loathed the fur bags even more.

By the time I crossed into the Buckeye State, my total trip mileage was a shade less than 5,000 miles. The constant bombardment of below-average temperatures, above-average winds and sodden skies had taken a toll on my wanderlust. I was feeling frayed.

The autumn-like chill in the morning air wasn't just my imagination working overtime. Minnesota, Wisconsin and Michigan had recorded near-record or record-breaking low temperatures for July. When I checked New York and Maine's weather, they were on the cool side of summer, too. For a guy whose nickname is "The Lizard," this was a concern.

I made a new game plan to go along with the conditions. I would resist the temptation to ride bonus miles in Ohio. For the first time in many states, I decided to head straight east. This would require me to hug the coastline of Lake Erie, placing me on a collision course with heavily populated Cleveland. However, on the Happy Meter, the Cleveland Indians baseball team had the same ETA as me. This was yin-yang cycling.

I took busy, wet highways into Toledo, which is named after the city in Spain. From the view on my approach, there was nothing European about it. On the outskirts were the usual big-box stores and shopping malls. Next came a plethora of used car dealerships, auto repair shops and light industry. This was followed closely by down-trodden neighborhoods with numerous "For Sale" signs on homes and some were just plain boarded-up. The road was as rough-and-tumble as the city.

I didn't entertain thoughts of retiring in the "Glass City."

For a few brief blocks the Toledo Museum of Art with its manicured parks, neoclassical buildings and gardens wowed me. The sight didn't last long enough as the funk returned all too quickly.

Obviously, Toledo's dependence on auto-parts manufacturing was taking its toll on the natives.

The downtown area showed signs of hope with lovingly restored old, brick buildings. I passed Fifth Third Field, which seemed to be the glue holding it all together. By that time the inclement weather had passed. There was no doubt that the Mud Hens would "play ball" that evening.

Soon after I was reacquainted with Dick at a sad and weathered Day's Inn. It appeared to be way past its prime, like the city around it. You know it's a rough place when a sign behind the check-in announces: "No parties will be tolerated in the rooms!"

I showered the muck off and quaffed a few brews that Dick was kind enough to supply. Faster than one can say "Holy Toledo!" we were off to see the Mud Hens.

Dick wanted to dine at Tony Packos, which is famous for hot dogs and Corporal Klinger from the TV show M.A.S.H. Despite my no-hot dog, no-beef, no-sausage approach to healthy eating, I followed him in. Who was I to argue with a 76-year-old classic? I make it a point to respect my elders, too.

After an underwhelming and overpriced meal, we scored two tickets for only $18 a short toss from the Hen's dugout. Now, that's a deal!

It wasn't much of a game. The home team's pitcher was henpecked by the Gwinnett Braves 6-zip in the first inning. That was as good as it got for the local heroes. Watching the carnage unfold was not a high priority. I was beat from my wet ride; Dick was tired from his wet drive. So we left before the final out. It was a nice stadium, even though the product was off.

In the morning, I said goodbye to my pony-tailed friend. A few miles later, I rejoined another old friend – Highway 2. A muggy, blasting tailwind pushed me along the lakeside. In the distance, I spotted the all-too-familiar shape of a nuclear power plant. The Davis-Besse plant once took a direct hit from a tornado and kept right on ticking. A human error later led to the plant closing for a year. Leave it to mankind to do what Mother Nature could not accomplish.

A majority of the plant's property is part of the National Wildlife Refuge system. I looked around for any eerily glowing or misshapen animals, but I am happy to say none was spotted.

I arrived in Port Clinton (self-proclaimed Walleye Capital of the World) and got a good look at Lake Erie. It's the fourth largest by surface area of the Great Lakes and smallest by volume. From my viewpoint, it looked pretty big. When a fierce wind whips from west to east, it can produce major differences in the water level on each side of the lake. The record is a whopping 16 feet. Buffalo, N.Y., can get flooded while Toledo is high and dry. This phenomenon has a cool name – seiches. I witnessed a few white caps but nothing dramatic.

Port Clinton and the nearby island of Put-in-Bay have a reputation for being the summer equivalent of spring break in Daytona Beach. I asked a local about the island. His response: "There's booze, lots of booze, girls and booze out there." You know you are getting old when hearing those words makes you retreat seven miles farther to a quieter neighborhood. Who would have thought there would come a time when a good night's rest sounded more inviting than ogling coeds?

I woke refreshed and knew I made the right choice. Seriously, how many young women would be warm to a guy their dad's age, anyway?

Summer had returned to western Ohio along with a fearsome tailwind. I got back on Highway 2 and crossed over the Thomas A. Edison Bridge. (He was born in nearby Milan.) Now I am not proud of this, but pedaling over that bridge is illegal. Bicycles are strictly verboten. I took a chance instead of a massive detour, but did not end up in cuffs.

I peeled off Highway 2 the first chance I got and took relaxed roads past lush sloughs to Sandusky. I was wrong again in assuming the city was named for a famous Polish immigrant. It's an Anglicized version of an Indian word meaning "cold water."

Shipping and manufacturing are on the wane in this Lake Erie shoreline city. Sandusky manufactures screams and fun at the nearby Cedar Point Amusement Park. Another thrill it produced in its varied past was freedom. Many homes in Sandusky were stations on the Underground Railroad during the Civil War. That firebrand Harriet Beecher Stowe named Sandusky the "gate to freedom" in "Uncle Tom's Cabin."

I took a coffee break in its Old Town area, where Doug approached me on his bicycle. He was a 74-year-old gent wearing a droopy tank top that matched an extra fold of skin around his middle. His Schwinn Paramount was half his age. That's an old bike. He told me how he lost 50 pounds just by riding his clunker around Sandusky. We made small talk about diet, exercise and cycling as I sipped my brew. Apparently, this retired propane dealer was quite a man-about-town as well. He greeted many citizens by their first names.

"Are you the mayor of Sandusky?" I asked.

"Nah! I just like meeting people."

He volunteered to lead me out of the harbor town through tree-lined, blue-collar residential neighborhoods. Before we parted ways, I suggested it might be time for an upgrade on his steed.

"Doug! A new bike would last you the rest of your life." He said he'd think about it.

From there it was a wonderfully short jaunt to my day's stopover in Vermilion. Once again, I'd be the guest of a family from the Warm Showers List. (I wish they would change that name.)

Before meeting my hosts, I set off to explore Vermilion. The lakeside town sits halfway between Toledo and Cleveland. Apparently, it's a prime location for marinas and the pleasure crafts that dock in them. The older neighborhoods possess a pampered appearance and the pride of local boosters can be seen throughout this city of 11,000.

If you ever find yourself there, make sure to pay a visit to the Inland Sea Museum. I guarantee you will gain $6 (entry fee) worth of smarts in a short time. The museum houses many exhibits about the ships that plied those waters. The subject matter includes navigation and ship building to those unfortunate vessels that have "gone missing." At 5 p.m., the curator came by to say the museum was closing. Too bad; there was plenty more to see in this gem of a place.

Sam, Susan and son Taylor were just a stone's throw from Highway 6. Perfect. As usual, I picked up a variety of good-faith offerings at a local grocery. I bought beer for the p.m. and coffee for the a.m. I reckoned one of those beverages would make anyone happy. I was wrong once when the hosts turned out to be a Mormon family. (Boy, was I embarrassed!)

My Ohioan hosts lived in an upper middle-class neighborhood in a spacious home. Susan was a dedicated teacher on summer break. I watched as she phoned a few of her wayward pupils about missing football or track practices.

Her reasoning for the off-duty vigilance was this: "Keeping those kids focused on sports helps keep them out of trouble. Most of my students live in the poor neighborhoods of Lorain. Many of them are being raised by their grandmothers. If they have one involved parent, this sets them apart from their peers."

It was a sad commentary on family life in northern Ohio. However, caring humans like Susan provide a dollop of hope for the future.

Her husband, Sam, is an osteopath. He chips in with the good deeds by providing free physical exams to budding athletes so they can stay on their teams if their parents cannot afford the luxury of a doctor's visit.

I was touched by the goodness in these generous acts. Maybe it does take a village to raise a child.

On another fine, blue-sky and warm morning, I departed after a few bracing cups of Sam's special blend coffee. (He home-roasts the beans himself.) I plan on keeping these Good Samaritans in the loop of my whereabouts and hope that one day I would be able to repay their kindness.

I turned east on Highway 6 toward Cleveland. I passed Lorain and lakeside mansions became the standard building type. Some of them were Walmart sized, big enough to house a small town.

While viewing the McMansions, I was practically pulled over by a fellow cyclist – Mick, the cop. He is a part-time triathlete and a full-time police officer in Cleveland.

He was curious in a professional way about what I was up to. He had a definite opinion concerning the Warm Showers List.

"I'm not sure if I would be OK with a stranger in my house," he said.

I tried reasoning with him: "What would a cyclist take? A flat-screen TV?"

I told him about the time I left a house key for a cross-country rider who needed a place to crash. I hid the key and told her where it was. I was in another state at the time. He looked at me as if I were born moments ago.

"You know, there are lots of bad people out there."

I would hazard a guess that Mick watches Fox News 24/7. When we parted ways, he said, "Be careful in Cleveland. Make sure to watch your back." I suppose that is sound, if paranoid, advice wherever you go.

Cleveland was founded in 1796, prior to Ohio becoming a state in 1803. Surveyors working around the area named it after their boss – Gen. Moses Cleaveland. (Talk about suck-ups.) Cleaveland came up with a downtown scheme based upon a public square, which still stands. He then left, never to be seen in Ohio again.

Could he have foreseen the decline of Cleveland's manufacturing and with it a sizable portion of its population? Maybe he was just scared away by its ranking as the 11th most dangerous city in the United States, according to the 2008 Morgan Quinto Press crime statistics.

Or did he have a bad feeling about Cleveland's Cuyahoga River, infamous for being "the river that caught on fire" in 1969 and 12 times prior to that. As a result of this manmade calamity, the Clean Water Act became law in 1972.

That old saying, "For every action, there's an opposite and equal reaction." might describe this event.

I knew right away when I crossed into Cleveland proper. The pleasant sounding street names in suburban Lakewood yielded to a functional yet boring numbering system. The city began in the West 170s. My goal was to survive to West 25th and turn inland away from the lake. The neighborhoods varied from upscale to funky to just plain seedy.

I was en route to another Warm Showers List stay. I contacted Lois to see if she would be interested in a visitor and a Cleveland Indians baseball game. As luck would have it, Lois and her boyfriend, Chris, were planning a baseball outing. They would be chaperoning a gaggle of neighborhood kids to a Tribe's game on the day of my arrival. She even picked up a ticket for me and, yes, I could be her guest, too. SCORE!

Lois' home was a rose amidst many thorns. The crash pad next door was boarded up and trashed. Down the block, a fire and ambulance station seemed to run calls non-stop. Nearby, a rust-bucket of a vehicle had an anti-theft device on its steering wheel, a sure sign of how desperate life in Cleveland had become.

Despite all those signs of squalor, Lois maintained a Pollyannaish outlook on it all.

"So many folks left Cleveland because of the down turn; it's now safe to ride a bike in rush-hour traffic. There are not as many cars as before!"

God bless the optimist.

She also had taken early retirement and founded the "Walk-Roll" organization, a non-profit gig to promote "human-powered neighborhood events that combine fun with active living, learning and participation." Great concept. This is a woman who radiates goodness.

After meeting my hostess, I dropped off my bike, cleaned up, paid Lois for the baseball ticket and left for downtown. I would meet her and her crew later.

I caught a bus toward Moses Cleaveland's idea of what a city center should to be. From the public square to the harbor and points in between, I'd say he did a swell job. If that visionary were alive today, I think he would be quite pleased with the results.

He may be gone but not forgotten. In the main square, Cleaveland scored a larger-than-life-sized statue. The local brewpub honored him with "Holy Moses White Ale." Personally, I'd rather be immortalized by a beer name instead of a statue for pigeons to poop on, but that's just me.

I spent the day wandering around the harbor marveling at the Rock and Roll Hall of Fame and Museum. Huey Lewis and the News sang, "The heart of rock and roll is in Cleveland," so it must be right. Actually, there is a grain of truth to the hype. In 1951, local DJ Alan Freed (also known as Moondog) coined the phrase rock 'n' roll to describe the upbeat rhythm and blues music he spun.

Resting peacefully next door to the Hall of Fame is the 618-foot bulk carrier steamship William G. Mather. Before its retirement in 1980, it gained notoriety in WWII for leading a convoy of freighters through the iced-choked waters of Lake Superior. Its mission was to pick up a load of iron ore from Duluth for the production of war materials.

After taking a couple of photos of this WWII hero, I ventured into the Great Lakes Science Center. It might have been misnamed. The center featured many educational exhibits, although none of them had anything to do with the Great Lakes. The closest they came to water was an IMAX film about the Colorado River.

After furthering my education at the museum and a few pre-game Happy Hour beers, I was ready to meet Lois and company for the Indians/Texas Rangers match up.

Progressive Field (car insurance) was built in 1994. I prefer the local's name for it – Jacobs Field, after the former team owners. A quick lap around this green lovely and I understood why it was ranked numero uno in the 2008 Sports Illustrated fan poll.

I found my seat next to Lois, Chris, four neighborhood tykes and Fred. It didn't take long for Fred to warm up to me as he launched into his bicycle resume and stories about his former military career. Evidently, this retired Marine sergeant was used to speaking without interruption. It was a grand thing that I am able to listen, drink beer and watch baseball at the same time. The conversation was mostly an entertaining monologue.

While in the service, Fred was on hand at the funerals of many former presidents. A Marine must be up on his spit and polish to score such a prestigious detail.

Fred sported a slight paunch and chin stubble. He kept busy riding around Cleveland and dabbling about on the Underground Railroad Trail. I enjoyed his story about the "No Smoking" signs that were once posted adjacent to the flammable Cuyahoga River.

The Indians went on to score one of their infrequent victories. I felt like we were all winners, especially the neighborhood kids.

I had trouble sleeping that night with all the police, fire and ambulance sirens going off in all directions from Lois' home. All those calls and it was only a Tuesday night. I'd hate to think of what the call load would be on a full-moon Friday night.

After a pancake breakfast and a round of goodbyes to Lois the Do-Gooder, I continued eastward. It was going to be a short day to Eastlake for another ballgame.

I was following Lois' directions on a bike-friendly route out of the city when I heard a minor explosion. My rear tire had been harpooned by a three-inch spike. This was no simple tube repair: This was a dead-in-the-water parts replacement of both tube and tire.

I phoned Lois for guidance. She went to work right away, Googling the closest bicycle shop.

"There's one a short walk from you. It's called Fridrich's. I'll phone ahead for you and see if they can help. What is your tire size?"

I felt like I had called the bicycle equivalent of AAA dispatch center.

A few minutes later, Lois was directing me in. Her parting words were, "The bike shop is kind of old and different." I didn't care just as long as they had replacement rubber.

The shop was in a gamier part of Cleveland. I pushed my wounded steed past locals partaking in brown-bag beers on the street at 9 a.m. A skinny homeless woman shuffled by me wearing mismatched shoes. She stopped to pick through the detritus of garbage cans along her aimless way. I was getting a feeling Fridrich's would not be selling top-of-the-line Treks.

I knocked on the gated front door. A mechanic smoking a cigarette allowed me an early entry. He then handed me off to Harold, who began searching through heaps of dusty tires for an elusive 700x28 touring tire.

"Found one!" he announced. "Here's a brand the cops use, so it must be OK."

With his task completed, he ambled outside for a cigarette break. Before his light-up he passed me off to Burt, who completed the task at hand. I asked him the obvious question: "How old is this place?"

"Fridrich's is over 100 years old." (It was founded in 1883.)

I glanced around the antique shop half expecting to see Orville and Wilbur Wright emerge from a back room. The inventors of the flying machine were once humble bike mechanics in Ohio.

I chatted with Burt as the master mechanic completed the repair. He made a sincere confession to me: "I once dreamed of riding cross-country but work, family and now old age got in my way. I admire guys like you who are getting it done."

I thanked him and paid another cigarette-smoking clerk for the job. After this unplanned detour, I got back on course.

I was intrigued by what I saw when crossing over the Hope Memorial Bridge, which is named after Bob Hope's dad. There was a set of Egyptian-like statues aptly named the "Guardians of Traffic." All four of the hulking studs held some type of vehicle in their muscular arms, although none out of the four cradled a bicycle. What would Mr. Fridrich say about this oversight?

I followed the Lake Erie shoreline for 28 miles to Eastlake. By the look of the traffic congestion and hyper-human activity, I was still in Cleveland. A few hours later I hailed a cab to go see the Lake County Captains take on the Augusta (Georgia) GreenJackets.

A sparse and subdued crowd was on hand to watch the home team fail. I would have thought with the mass of humanity around these parts, the stadium would have been jammed. So much for my guessing.

I got an early start to avoid rush-hour traffic. Luckily, I was heading against the grain. It wasn't too bad on Highway 20. It would have been a grand ride if your idea of scenery were strip malls and big-box stores.

In Mentor, a brown National Park Service sign grabbed my attention. The former home of President James Garfield beckoned me across the highway. It was too early for the park to be officially open, but security was lax. I pedaled around the compound reading informative signs about America's 20th president. I felt like I was riding on hallowed grounds.

I saw the front porch of Mr. Garfield's home, which played an important role in his presidential campaign. Supporters came to his residence to ask questions and visit. Now with the presidential campaign beginning two years prior to that first Tuesday in November, I say bring back the good old days.

Garfield, who was a bookish man, held office a mere four months before he was assassinated by a deranged gunman. From what I read about him, he might have turned out to be one of our better presidential choices. He died two months shy of turning 50 years old.

I was barely awake when I scored this American history lesson. Not a bad way to start the day.

Farther east outside of Painesville (Why would anyone want to live in a place named that?) I pulled over to check out an off-road fruit stand. While squeezing peaches for ripeness, I met Anne and her two kids. She had an attractive Farrah Fawcett-like look minus the big hair. Her little ones were respectful, well-behaved and full of questions. "What's this for? Why do you carry water? What's in this pack?"

Anne asked the usual adult questions: "Where did you start? Where are you going?"

She offered me a handful of blueberries as she kept a watchful eye on her brood. Anne's kids didn't know it, but they were lucky. Their parents really cared about them.

After this pleasant interlude, I returned to the Lake Erie shore passing through Geneva-on-the-Lake. It's a resort town whose claim to fame is being the first post-Civil War vacation spot in the country. Now it has a honky-tonk feel with tattoo parlors, video arcades and biker bars that are not the pedaling kind. Those war-weary veterans wouldn't recognize the place.

I gained State Route 531, which is part of the National Scenic Byways program. The road afforded me glimpses of the lake. A few pleasure boats drifted lazily on the vast pond. The scene was tranquil enough to lower a person's blood pressure.

Ashtabula contained a working blue-collar port and heaps of older homes and businesses. Another National Park Service sign directed my attention to Hubbard's House. The residence was once another station on another track of the Underground Railroad. Ship captains with consciences would ferry the escaped slaves to Canada. There must have been something in Lake Erie's water that made citizens go out of their way to perform not-so-random acts of kindness.

In Conneaut, my plan to spend a night on the lakeside went askew due to a full hotel. While exiting the town, I noticed appealing older homes going for the price of a low-end luxury auto. I had passed through this quaint Midwest town the previous summer while heading west and saw its better days. The speed of the economic decline was depressingly apparent.

Back on Highway 2, a few more miles took me out of Buckeye State.

Part Way in Pennsylvania

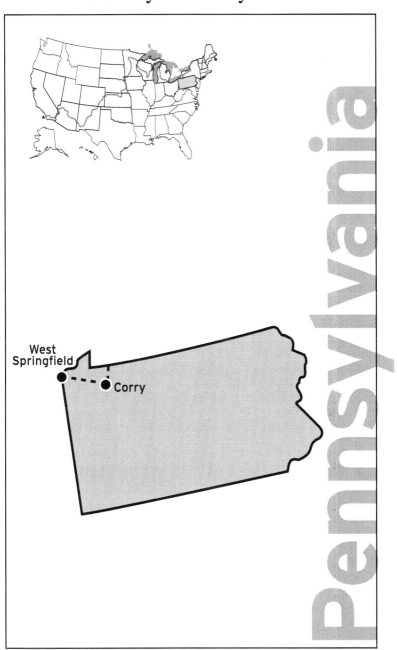

14. Part Way in Pennsylvania

"Engine 6! Eastside ambulance! Larimer County sheriff's deputies request your assistance on an elderly assault victim at …"

We headed east into the rural area surrounding Fort Collins. Eastside ambulance had arrived ahead of us and was already giving aid to the senior citizen. I was the lead EMT that shift and began assisting the paramedics.

The victim was someone's grandma with her grayish-white hair matted down from congealed blood. She had multiple scalp wounds. She was conscious, but shell-shocked from what she had endured.

Apparently, a few young thugs attempted to break into her home believing the place was unoccupied. She surprised them and paid the price for it. The scumbags went at her with a baseball bat. It was a testament to her strength and will that she still able to speak.

We staunched the bleeding and loaded her into the ambulance. She appeared stable enough that the paramedics did not require an extra hand. We were released from the scene.

On our way back to the station, I felt pretty shaken by what I had just seen: A senseless act of incredible violence inflicted upon a helpless elderly person. My fellow crew members didn't appear to be bothered by what we had witnessed. For them, it was business as usual. Their lack of compassion showed the hardening that comes from the world of emergency services.

I can honestly say that to the day I retired, a call dealing with such cruelty bothered me.

I stopped at the first hotel I came to in Pennsylvania, which is named after that British Quaker, William Penn. I was feeling roughed up by a lack of solid rest and decided a short day was in order.

Home for the evening was the west side of Springfield. My hotel's back door was practically on the shoulder of Interstate 90. Despite the constant drone of traffic, it was a great location. The Springside Bar and Grill was right next door.

I immediately liked the place when I saw that a patron had parked his tractor outside. I bet that farm implement was a unique chick magnet. Imagine the conversation: "Let's take a ride on my tractor and head out to Lover's Lane!"

I slid through the smoky atmosphere and found an empty stool by the bar. Bonnie came by and took my order. Behind her was a list of locals who had been 86ed from the joint for life. Evidently, the Wilsons, Halls and Grahams were a wild bunch. Each last name was mentioned three times.

I had to ask: "Bonnie, what does one have to do to get kicked out of here for life?"

Her answer was short and to the point: "A lot!"

She then added: "Fighting will do it all the time. A few of those guys are down to one bar between two states."

I explained that no matter how much I drink, I'm always 5-feet-4. I don't get any stronger, larger or tougher with alcohol.

She smiled at that and said, "The young guys could learn from you."

I woke rejuvenated and ready to head into the Pennsylvania hills. The Allegheny Mountains were an unknown area to me, so I felt it was worthy of a bonus-miles detour. It was an eight-mile uphill slog from the Lake Erie shoreline to Albion and breakfast. The easy-on-the-wallet menu spoke heaps about the lack of cash in this remote corner of the Keystone State. It's a shame the fine-looking hardwood forests and rolling beauty didn't equate to prosperity.

I dropped down into a valley and into the busyness of Edinboro, a regional center for goods and services. A few miles farther east, Union City stood at the opposite end of the economic spectrum. The town had a bleak, sad and gray look along its main arteries. Even the sole motel in town was out of business. I pressed on and upward toward Corry.

There I ran into the classic cycle tourist dilemma. Should I suck it up for another 30 miles and three hours of slow motion or put a fork in it and call the day done? At a Subway sandwich place, I decided lunch and a map break were in order.

Just then a mother and daughter, Dee and Ashley, bounded toward me on their mountain bikes. They were blond, wore tank tops, running shorts and toothpaste-commercial smiles. I thought this must have been a mother-daughter cheerleader tryout. They made the usual inquiries and got the lowdown on me in no time. They strongly suggested Corry as the place to be, even for just one night.

"It's a great town. We love it here. It's safe, and the people are friendly." They demonstrated this point by adding, "If you come to our bar and grill tonight, we'll buy you dinner."

Talk about a welcome wagon.

I said a temporary goodbye to mom and daughter and went in search of a place to lay my head for the night. A quick look-see of the downtown wowed me. Post Civil War brick buildings were adorned with colorful murals. Civil pride went as far as a new coat of paint for the structures. However, like a date who applied too much makeup, a glance was deceiving. Most of the stores in those lovely buildings were vacant.

At dinnertime I strolled over to the Corner Bar for my promised meal. Mike the bartender, also the owner and Dee's brother, dropped an icy beer before me. Ashley took my meal order and handed it to Dee, the cook. Between cooking dinners for the masses, Dee introduced me to her mom, Debbie.

Debbie came by and chatted while I waited for my meal.

"This town once had 10,000 people living here. Now there's about 6,400. The jobs are disappearing." She took a sip on her whiskey sour and said wistfully, "I wish we could go back to the way it was in the '50s and '60s when this country made things."

While Debbie was on the subject of local history, I questioned her about the firefighter memorial on Main Street.

"That was in 1970: A paint store exploded and five poor fellows were killed. My sister-in-law's son was one of those firefighters. My sister-in-law and the community weren't right for some time." She went on to reminisce about happier days until duty called her away.

After my splendid meal of poached cod and veggies, I asked for the check. "Nope!" Dee said, "Our pleasure."

I couldn't in clear conscience take advantage of such generosity, so I dropped a super-sized tip for Ashley. I hoped it would become part of her college fund.

After a few patio beers in other parts of downtown, I ventured back to the only B&B in Corry. I passed out into Neverland almost immediately. Around 2ish I heard a commotion, took a bathroom break and returned to Dreamland.

I woke early to jump start my day riding through the Allegheny National Forest. I fired up the coffee pot as two fellow B&B guests wandered into the dining room. A 20-something-girl was keeping a wary eye on her boyfriend. His shirt was covered in dried blood and his nose was left of center. She poured two cups of Joe and handed one to her boyfriend, who was inhaling cigarettes outside. Here was the source of my past-midnight wake up call. Someone had apparently clocked this guy.

She returned inside after her java delivery. I went into EMT mode: "Did he lose consciousness after being punched?"

"I don't think so."

"Has he been repeating the same question over and over?"

"Not more than usual."

"Does he have a severe headache?"

"He has migraines every day."

I was beginning to see a pattern: Could those migraines be hangovers?

Before taking leave, I left her with some grownup advice. "Your boyfriend will eventually find out that he is not the biggest badass in town. There will come a time when another dude won't settle a fight with just his fists. Try to talk some sense into him before he becomes a crime statistic."

I saw in her boyfriend a "dead man walking." It wasn't a matter of if; it was a matter of when.

I felt weary from the previous day's climbs and anticipated more of the same. But it wasn't so bad. I was in the Alleghany River valley, whose waters contribute significantly to the formidable Ohio River. The Alleghany Plateau is also famous for fostering the world's first oil boom. It all began in Titusville, just southwest of where I was pedaling.

From my vantage point on Highway 6, I saw cornfields dotted with spent mini-oil derricks rusting away in the Pennsylvania elements and serving as interesting lawn ornaments.

In Warren, the stench of petroleum permeated the air. The smell came upriver from the United Refining Co. plant. Even with fetid air, a guy needs to eat. After taking a second breakfast in a rather nice downtown, I crossed a bridge over the Alleghany River.

Below the bridge a non-motorized boat race was in full flight. Paddler in canoes and kayaks attacked the river with frenzied strokes. I had no idea where the fast-paced race was heading or where it began. I was just pleased not to be involved. It looked like too much work for my road-weary body.

I then realized my steed was sick. The front chain ring shifter wasn't doing its job, leaving me stuck in the granny gears. Upon closer inspection, I found the cable had worn away and needed replacement. Those easy gears would have been appropriate for the Alps or Rockies, but not so much in Pennsylvania. I would have truly been spinning my wheels with little gain.

I returned to Warren and found a bike shop six miles in the opposite direction of my travel. Cross-country tours require flexibility. While the patient mechanic worked on my injured companion, I developed a new plan.

I decided to leave Pennsylvania a day earlier than planned. Those lovely and undiscovered (to me) Alleghany Mountains would have to wait. My new destination was up north to Jamestown, N.Y., and the state where I was born.

The silver lining was the Jamestown Jammers baseball club would be in town, too.

Northeast in New York

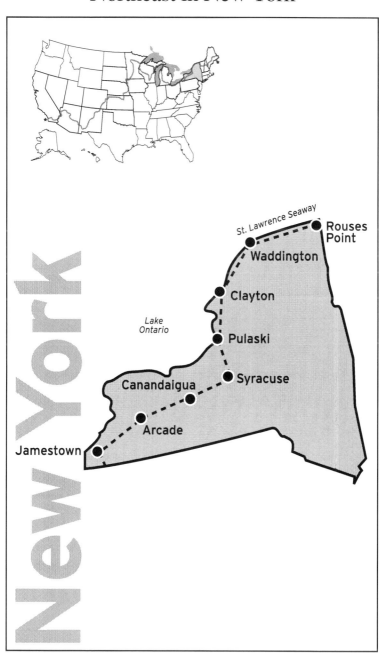

15. Northeast in New York

"Engine Two! Westside ambulance! Report of an unresponsive 85-year-old man at ..."

We high-tailed it to the address and found an elderly and rather calm woman pointing at her husband in a La-Z-Boy recliner with his legs propped up. It didn't require a doctor to know he was falling into the great beyond.

Ken "Action" Jackson the paramedic grabbed the inert body (not too gently) out of the chair and placed him (not too gently) on the living room floor. After all, medics cannot perform CPR on a guy chillin' in a La-Z-Boy. Like a scene from a movie, the impact of the old timer striking the ground had a miraculous effect. He came to.

"What are you doing to me? Why are you in my house?" he sputtered.

After explaining what had occurred to the disbelieving senior citizen, we took him to the hospital for further evaluation.

From that day on, we always asked paramedic Ken to teach us the "Action-Jackson-Full-Body-Slam Precordial Thump." He would usually blush, grin and shake his head.

Jamestown is noted for being the birthplace of Lucille Ball, although she denied it. (She told people she was born in Butte,

Mont.) I rode past the post office where a gigantic stamp featuring Lucy and Ricky highlighted the building. The city goes so far as to sponsor a "Lucy Fest" in August. How often would one hear those immortal words – "Lucy! You've got some 'splaining to do!" – that weekend?

The city once prided itself as the Furniture Capital of the World, but most of the wood-working plants had migrated away by 2009. These days, a Cummings diesel engine plant keeps the economy somewhat revved up. As my luck would have it, Cummings was generous enough to sponsor the Jammers vs. Aberdeen (Maryland) IronBirds game. This equated to free tickets.

After checking into the most overpriced, undervalued and shabby motel of my entire trip (I won't name names – it was a Red Roof Inn.) I went to Russell Diethrick Park for the contest. It was a fairly basic stadium with an approachable working-man's feel about it. Even with free tickets, only one-third of the seats were occupied. The crowd was polite and subdued for a Saturday night. I had a gut feeling the organization was doing its best just to stay afloat.

I made it to the seventh inning stretch and joined the spectators in a not-so-rousing rendition of "Take Me Out to the Ballgame." It was then time for this cyclist to find his bed.

The hotel had fidgety guests tinkering about in the night, making sleep uneven and broken. The one amenity this rip-off joint had was a coffee machine in the lobby. I visited it five times for lattes to jump start my day.

A warm, sauna-like fog greeted me that Sunday morning. The mist collected on my eyebrows and helmet as I passed swamplands complete with lily pads and submerged trees. As the sun broke through, the temperature rose accordingly. As the McDonald's commercial reminds us, "I'm lovin' it."

I was in serious need of calories by the time I arrived in Randolph. I secured my bike to a gas meter at the R&M Diner. The waitress was smiley and quick; a wonderful combo for a hungry cyclist.

Hal and Ron sat at an adjacent table. All it took was for me to ask one question about directions. Ron gave me the direct, easy-to-follow route. But Hal, a big man with big opinions, said, "Nope! That's not the way to go. Take Toad Road to East Otto to Orchard Place to …"

Following him on my map I realized all the bonus miles I would have to cover. "Hal! Have you been smoking rope? That would be completely out of my way to Syracuse."

He looked almost hurt: "Well, I was trying to keep you from riding up Murder Hill."

I tried to be gentle on this non-cyclist as I explained, "All hills come to an end or else all roads would lead to Mount Everest."

Western New York is a mini-Ireland when it comes to water elements. H2O was my constant companion as it gurgled, flowed or lay stagnant. It existed on the opposite side of the water table compared to the arid Southwest.

Upon arrival in aptly named Little Valley, I met Lisa and Alice strolling on a walkway with cigarettes in hand. Alice looked me and my bike over and said, "I'd love to do something like that one day."

It was my turn to play Jewish mother on them. "Bad girls! Bad girls! Don't you know that cigarette smoking is unhealthy? How are you going to ride with me if you smoke?"

Embarrassed by my outburst, they both snuffed out their cancer sticks. Lisa blurted out, "We're quitting in September!"

"Fine! Then you can meet me somewhere near my finish line."

They giggled at the thought. As I rode away, I was pretty certain they were fibbing about giving up the nasty habit.

After Little Valley things got serious on Hal's "Murder Hill." The real name is not as dramatic – McCarthy Hill. Yes, it was a grind, but lots easier than riding the 3,000 bonus miles Hal had suggested. I couldn't complain about the sweat power needed to get to the top. The views made up for the effort and then some. Upstate New York really is a green gem.

From that hill's summit I tumbled down through Ellicottville, a ski resort town minus the snow. It seemed to be a cool town with relaxed folks sipping caffeine at outdoor cafes. I wanted to join them, but, as usual, to quote Robert Frost, I had "miles to go before I sleep."

First I had to attend to a small bike maintenance issue. My tires were on the soft side of rolling resistance. I pulled into a local bike shop for a floor pump fix and met Josh a moment later.

"Dude! Years ago I said 'no way' to riding cross-country. Now I am Jones-in to do it. What's it like?"

"Dude! You better enjoy riding a bike each and every day for long periods of time. If you do, I think you would love it. We live in a great country and its best seen from a bicycle."

He shook his head in an affirmative motion. I don't think he ran out and bought a touring bike, though.

I continued on Highway 242, eventually bumping into busy Highway 16. One more turn on 39 placed me in the village of Arcade and I was done for the day. It must have been ol' Murder Hill because I felt whooped. I got to bed early to prepare for an 86-mile stint featuring predicted highs in the 90s and humidity the next day.

I mapped out a route to Canandaigua that looked both direct and promising. I was barely out of Arcade when I must have missed a turn. Somehow the roads and the map weren't matching up. I knew I was heading east by that big shiny orb in my eyes. The immortal words of baseball sage, Yogi Berra came to mind: "We're lost but we are making good time!" I quickly came up with an alternative plan to head to Warsaw. (Not Poland: I wasn't that lost.)

A gauzy haze lay in the valleys creating outstanding photo ops. The landscape switched between fields of soybeans and corn and forests. They were pleasant roadside companions. It was literally a plunge into Warsaw, an incredible 10 percent grade in an area that sees long periods of ice and snow. The number of wintertime wrecks must keep the local volunteers firefighters hopping.

Once again I shifted plans and turned north on Highway 19, following the Oatka Creek drainage. If I had continued east, I would have had to gear down and deal with a 10 percent grade to exit that valley. Isn't it funny how things work that way?

On Highway 20/5 the miles rolled along with the peaks and valleys of the highway. By the time I arrived in the Finger Lake city of Canandaigua, my legs were toast from the day's ups and downs.

Canandaigua has a multi-tiered history consisting of Indians, treaties, steamships, and the Women's Rights Movement. I am not sure how these wide-ranging events were ever connected, but somehow they took place around this city. These days Canandaigua Lake provides the wet resource to make it a prime resort area in central New York State.

I wound up at Jose and Willy's Bar and Grill, where I drank warm beer while a fan blew tepid, grease-laden vapors around the joint. The bar had a bay window overlooking the lake. From my stool I watched as a salmon-colored sunset compensated for the lack of amenities.

I still felt drained when I woke and was in dire need of coffee. I staggered the few feet to the Lafayette Diner and took a seat at the counter. I was the only non-local there. Gary provided too-early entertainment by reading bad jokes from a Reader's Digest to a groaning crowd. For the under-caffeinated in the restaurant (me), this was a painful experience. The lone waitress busied herself by playing interior decorator in the café. She was placing "Happy Birthday!" stringers along the walls. I guessed it was not meant for one of the patrons. It seemed pouring coffee and taking breakfast orders were low on her agenda. Once in awhile, an impatient customer would slam his cup down to get her attention. I wanted to shout at her, "Stay focused! Do your job!" but I kept my trap shut. I finally scored a few cups of Joe, but still felt spent. I was in need of a respite from the road.

My day's journey to Syracuse was no labor of love. I went through the motions with little joy while literarily passing through American history in the Finger Lakes area.

Waterloo was the birthplace of Memorial Day. Seneca Falls gave birth to the Women's Rights Movement. On a similar note, Amelia Bloomer, a noted teacher, feminist and publisher of America's first women's newspaper, lived there. Yes, she is also famous for provided us with another name for unmentionable undergarments – bloomers.

On the outskirts of Syracuse I dodged buses and irate male drivers en route to Tom and Hope's home. I was back in the city where I spent four long, cold and snowy winters while attending the State University of New York College of Environmental Science and Forestry. It is not a roll-off-the-tongue name.

I won't kid you: Barely 5-feet-1 when I arrived as a pony-tailed 17-year-old punk, I was a Little Man on Campus. (I had a growth spurt my freshman year that pushed me up to 5-feet-4.)

Tom and Hope were old college acquaintances who decided to call the Salt City home. Hope is a retired special education teacher whose mission in life is to make her home the envy of Martha Stewart. Tom is the handyman/carpenter who makes it happen. They are a duo who gets things done. When Tom isn't working on Hope's whims, he is making fine musical instruments and playing them, too. He manages to remain humble despite his many talents.

Tom is also a mellow Irishman who has a knack of seeing through people. He demonstrated that trait to me in quick time.

"Jeff! You look tired. I think you should hang out for a few nights and rest."

"You are so right. I need a break from the bike for my final push to Maine."

With that invitation I spent three days wandering around my old haunts in a dream-like state. That youth who once walked those streets, ate in those pizzerias and bought Genesee Cream Ale in the grocery stores seemed a stranger to me now. Author Thomas Wolfe was right: "You can't go home again."

The highlight of my trip down memory lane was having dinner with five of my former college chums. A few I hadn't seen in more than 30 years.

Married couple Mike and Maureen surprised me by showing up. Mike and I were roommates in an "Animal House" setting when we were sophomores. Mike now spends his days working for a soil and water conservation district. His passion besides Maureen is beekeeping. Maureen hasn't changed much with her wavy, auburn Celtic hair and long skirts. Her smile and good cheer are still omnipresent. She works as a labor and delivery nurse, which I find very appropriate. Together they've raised three very Irish-looking children.

Barb and Harvey tied the knot after their senior years. To me, they are an odd couple. Barb works at a Squibb Drug research center in the molecular biology field. She speaks in a chipped, precise fashion. She is brilliant. A long time ago, she was my dance partner in a 52-hour dance marathon fundraiser for Muscular Dystrophy. Harvey is a computer consultant who pauses between thoughts and sentences.

One must be patient when conversing with him. He can pluck a mean guitar.

Paul had the same warped grin and shock of hair. He's still an entertaining character. He makes his living working for the U.S. Department of Agriculture as an agronomist.

We laughed, reminisced and joked around. For those precious few hours, it felt like old times. At the end of an early evening, I sincerely thanked them for making the effort to visit with me. They eventually wandered back to their homes, jobs and family obligations. I wandered back to wandering.

After another round of goodbyes, I decided to become reacquainted with the bike for a short day of riding. At this point, I had seen four out of the five Great Lakes. I was within a few hours of Lake Ontario. Why not?

Half of my mileage was spent getting past Syracuse's metro area. The neighborhoods were blue-collar and barely holding their own. A few rougher areas had apparently tossed in the towel: "For Sale" signs were the standard instead of the exception.

Eventually I broke out into the country and was reminded what a lush and attractive state New York is. I experienced this feeling despite the gloomy skies and thick air.

In Mexico (New York, not the country), I chanced upon another hot bed of Underground Railroad activity. The town boasts two structures on the National Register of Historic Places that were former safe houses for slaves en route to freedom. I was beginning to understand there were many kind-hearted white folks in these

261

northern latitudes. I can only hope the god of karma paid them back in full – and then some.

At Selkirk Shores State Park, I turned off hectic Highway 3 and in an instant I was enveloped in silence and hardwoods. Ominous signs stated, "Beach. No Swimming!" I took a seat on a bench and gazed out over Lake Ontario. I had bicycled to all of the Great Lakes. I wished the Nine Point nuclear power plant were not in sight: Its cooling towers kind of ruined my moment of elation.

Lake Ontario is the smallest of the Great Lakes in terms of surface area, although it contains more volume than Lake Erie. For a guy from the landlocked and dry state of Colorado, it looked to me to be on the large side of impressive.

On the U.S. side of the lake, two million Americans live within its watershed. On the Canadian side, an impressive nine million souls live near its shores. To put it another way, one out of every four Canadians resides near this body of water. Lake Ontario might be the runt of the litter, but it still deserves our respect.

I called it a night in Pulaski. It didn't take me long to realize the local economy revolved around fish. Fishing guides, fish-cleaning services and bait-and-tackle shops dominated the scene. The highways were choked with weekend-warrior fishermen hauling well-equipped boats behind pickup trucks. This could possibly be one of the few places where the other visitors would wake before me. That evening I was quite happy no swimming creatures surfaced in my dreams.

Before leaving fish haven, I spotted two touring cyclists across the street at a convenience store. I wandered over to meet and greet them. James and Collin were on their inaugural tour, which was riding around Lake Ontario. They were young, focused and smart graduate students from prestigious Cornell University. They went as far as to call me "sir." Our short encounter gave me hope for their generation. The conversation never diverted toward Briteny Spears, Paris Hilton or the latest video game. We rode together to Henderson Harbor before parting ways. They were on a mission to cover 150 miles that day. I just wanted to survive half that distance to Clayton. I was once young, too.

In Sackets Harbor, I discovered its role in the War of 1812. In order to keep the pesky Brits and Canadians at bay, the fledging United States garrisoned a large contingent of soldiers and sailors along the lake shore. American war ships were constructed here in order to gain supremacy on Lake Ontario. Two major 1812 battles occurred on local soil, and both times the Americans repelled the invaders.

During WWII, another group of "invaders" found themselves in Sackets Harbor. This time the arrivals came in peace, unarmed and invited. The town was the site of the only refugee camp in the United States. For 18 months, 982 displaced people (mostly Jews) found a safe harbor from the horrors of Nazi-occupied Europe.

After the history lesson, I detoured through lovely flat countryside to Cape Vincent, another place rich in 1812 lore. It's also where Lake Ontario flows out to the sea via the St. Lawrence River. From my shoreline lookout, I saw Ontario, Canada, to the north. It struck me on how far I had come.

This was the start of the fabled Thousand Islands, which happens to be more than 1,800. I guess "1,800 Islands" doesn't roll off the tongue as well. Here the definition of an island can be something as insignificant as a gull's rocky perch or a real chunk of property in the range of thousands of acres. The island chain was once the playground of America's bluebloods. Now Canadians and Americans of all social strata share its scenic wealth.

I made it Clayton for the night. Clayton is the self-proclaimed geographic center of the Thousand Islands. It's an attractive resort town with an antique boat museum and a riverside boardwalk. Clayton is where the ubiquitous Thousand Island salad dressing (a garnish of questionable health merits) originated.

For me, my evening was made by the sight of an ocean-going freighter heading northeast toward the Atlantic. A purplish cloud enhanced the sunset over the St. Lawrence Seaway, a sight that would have made Ansel Adams take notice. I felt privileged to have been there for the celestial show.

On a no-need for sunglasses morning, I continued along the Seaway Trail toward Alexandria Bay. My internal fuel gauge was pegging empty as I pedaled into the Northern Café. A mid-life couple watched as I secured my steed.

"Are you familiar with the Warm Showers List?" they asked. "We are listed as hosts for Rome, New York. Would you care to join us for breakfast?"

Larry and Patty were vacationing in the Thousand Islands. Neither of them were hardcore cyclists by any means; just gracious humans willing to allow pannier-laden bicyclists to spend a night. We exchanged notes on what it's like to be on the giving and receiving end of the WSL. When I told them about always picking up a few offerings for my generous hosts, their jaws dropped. "We've had 10 groups come through and not one of them dropped off anything more than a 'thank you!'"

I gently explained how my Jewish mother (may she rest in peace) would have been disappointed in me if I showed up empty-handed to a stranger's home. "She raised me better than that!"

It was a different breakfast break for me then staring at my maps. True to form, Larry picked up the check, like the gentleman he was. I paid the tip, like the gentleman I try to be.

On a sublimely silent stretch of Highway 12, I was overtaken by Ron. "I rode cross-country in 2000 with five other guys. We had all turned 65 that year," he said "That's how we celebrated. It kind of got boring toward the end."

Ron spent half the year on the shores of the St. Lawrence and the other half on the shore of the Atlantic Ocean in Florida.

"Now I can ride about 20 miles out and back these days. Hard to believe just nine years ago, I was able to ride across the U.S. A body can age quickly."

I made a mental note to hold onto this observation for my future use.

Ron turned back to Alexandria Bay for a nap. I continued east toward Ogdensburg.

A glance around the dumpy downtown showed this was no resort town. At best it was a down-and-dirty, blue-collar small city. Two state correctional institutions keep the local economy groaning along.

A sign on the outskirts of town made me pause to ponder. A left-pointing arrow indicated, "Bridge to Canada." Underneath that, a forward-facing arrow read, "Psychiatric Center." I had no choice: I left my passport at home. I proceeded straight ahead.

Shortly thereafter, I veered away from the St. Lawrence and into part of New York that's void of people. I was warned beforehand by Tom. "There are not a lot of humans in that part of our state." As usual, he was correct.

I was taking another detour for a date with my past to spend a night with another former college chum – Anne Johnson. She hadn't changed much in the quarter century since I'd seen her last. Her gapped-tooth smirk was the same, although her once red hair now had streaks of gray. Anne's love of green things translated to becoming a part-time wetlands botanist. She still spoke in a measured way, as her sentences evolved with each new thought. I always thought highly of her when we hung around in Syracuse.

She lived with her husband, Ted, in a new home on a remote county road. Ted is a handy guy who invents parts to be used for research and development projects at nearby Clarkson University. They were the proud parents of a virtual Noah's Ark of pets. Their children included one old hound, three cats, four birds, numerous gold fish and Tom the tortoise, who I almost stepped on. The only thing missing was a partridge in a pear tree.

Anne explained how her old home was burned to the ground by an errant bolt of lightning. She began many sentences with "before the house burned down …" or "when the house burned down …"

This evoked memories of my former career. We would do our job, put out the fire and walk away. We never realized the emotional baggage left in the ashes when someone loses their home. Maybe our salvage and overhaul should have included one more humane step.

One item Anne saved save was a box of old photos. "It's hard to believe they survived the fire." She said this as she presented me with three photos from my college days.

Who was that pony-tailed, unwrinkled idealistic youth? I stared at the proverbial stranger to myself. She generously handed them to me. "Just make sure you send them back after showing them off," she kindly asked. I promised her I would, and I did.

Before leaving, I invited this quirky couple to visit me out west. I knew I was just talking into space. Anne and Ted were certifiable homebodies. I ventured off with a twinge of envy for those fortunate souls who can attain happiness and contentment without the need for motion. It was a foreign concept to me.

Five miles of riding brought me back to the St. Lawrence River and the town of Waddington. Carp is king in this riverside community of 2,200. Forget those pesky walleye, trout and bass, these "gamers" liked their fish big, ugly and of the introduced-to-the-New-World variety. The local chamber of commerce goes so far as to sponsor a Junior World Carp Fishing Tournament. Watch for it live one day on ESPN.

I followed the Seaway Trail to the Eisenhower Lock. This and numerous other engineering marvels allow ocean-going crafts passage in and out of the Great Lakes. In my over-the-road method of travel, I had followed the movement from the final port in Duluth and Lake Superior to Lake Michigan to Lake Huron to Lake Erie and Lake Ontario and beyond. I'm pretty sure the freighters were able to cover the miles of the vast waterway in a shorter time frame than I did. I experienced less seasickness, though.

I stopped to give the lock a once over. A tourist-friendly security guard came out of a doublewide to speak to me: "Sorry to tell you, there won't be any freighters going through the lock today. With the downturn in the world economies, shipping is 40 percent down."

It wasn't my imagination after all; the sight of a Great Lakes freighter was as elusive as capturing the Loch Ness monster on film.

With a westerly tailwind urging me along and a drop in elevation to Lake Champlain., I decided to go long. I blew through towns with odd names such as Bombay and Constable. The farms I went by were more feral and disheveled than their Midwestern counterparts. The notion of a "place for everything and everything in its place" didn't hold water in these parts.

On the outskirts of Chateaugay, a multi-acre wind farm covering the ridgeline went about the business of providing green energy to the national grid.

A few miles later in Churubusco, I came across Dick's Country Store, Musical Oasis and Gun City all rolled into one. It looked like a gas station, but the sign advertised, "Dicks! Home of 1,000 guns and 500 guitars." Everything you would desire to fulfill your musical and firepower needs.

The miles piled on as I followed the Great Chazy River. At another border crossing, the red-and-white Maple Leaf flag fluttered adjacent to the Stars and Stripes. Quebec and Canada were directly to my north. In the nearby border towns, Canadian coins intermixed easily with U.S. greenbacks.

I crossed over Interstate 87 where a sign warned, "Last exit in the U.S." Another sign merely stated, "Montreal – 40 miles." In Champlain, I could almost smell the fine French-Canadian cuisine. Never mind: The odor was only a McDonald's serving up French fries from across the street.

I was on a downward slide to Lake Champlain when I completed my 110-mile day in Rouses Point. I was glad to be done.

My moldy (yet overpriced) hotel acted as a barometer for the town. The hotel sign advertised a resort, conference center and restaurant: All were missing. The empty pool contained weeds where water used to be. A stroll downtown verified my initial impressions. Those elegant old buildings contained nothing but empty store fronts.

The dinner-and-drink selection consisted of a take-it-or-leave-it variety. There was one bar and one take-away joint serving up pizza and greasy chicken parts. After ordering a beer, I questioned the bartender: "This town is not doing so well, is it?"

She mumbled a quiet, "No!" and turned her back to me. She was busy watching "Jeopardy" on TV.

The next day a Monet-blue sky greeted me as I said "good morning" once again to Highway 2. I rode my old buddy's shoulder up and over a bridge spanning a neck of Lake Champlain and into Vermont.

Very Little Time in Vermont

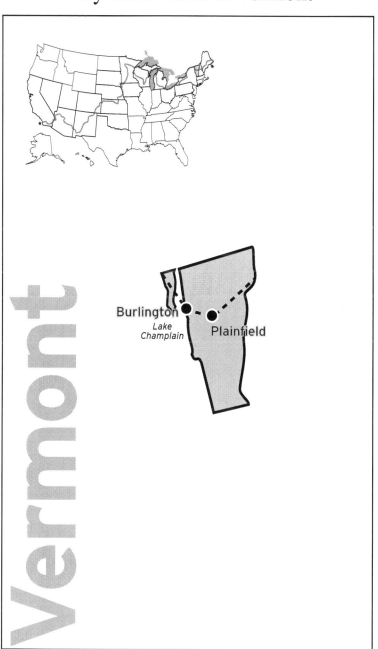

16. Very Little Time in Vermont

"Engine 5! Eastside ambulance! Respond to a report of a young man scalded after opening a radiator cap. Patient is located at …"

It was a toasty July day in my rookie year of firefighting. The location of the call was a gas station up the road from Station 5. My crew, one of many in my career, consisted of Captain Kirk and Steve, our driver operator. We arrived on scene in a flash. Steve was notorious for carrying a lead foot and secretly aspiring to be a NASCAR driver.

The victim, who was in his mid-20s, was writhing in a world of pain in the parking lot of a gas station. He had hardcore second-degree burns on his face and chest. He pleaded with bystanders to bring him some ice or cold water to quench the burn. About half a dozen people stood quietly around slurping on Slurpees, licking ice cream cones or just gazing at him. Not one of them responded to his cries for assistance.

We punched a few ice packs to activate the chemical reaction and gingerly placed them on his reddish wounds. We wrapped him mummy fashion in a sterile sheet. Once the sheet was in place, we cooled him further with an application of sterile water. We made sure he didn't start to shiver. The paramedics began to perform their magic with IVs and painkillers.

Once we had him stabilized, he asked, "Why didn't anyone help me? All they did was watch."

My boss, Kirk, placed a hand on his shoulder and gently said, "Son, people are strange. You never know how they will react in an emergency."

That short speech rang true for the next 27 years of emergency service work for me.

I was barely past the bridge into Vermont when Fort Montgomery caught my roving eye. Back in the early 1800s, when international tensions were running high, the fort was constructed on what was assumed to be U.S. territory. Wrong!

It was soon christened Fort Blunder when officials discovered it was built on the Quebec side of the fence. It turned out to be a well-mannered structure of war. A cannon or rifle shot was never fired from its ramparts.

On Highway 2, I did time on the Lake Champlain Scenic Byway and its Chain of Lakes segment. It was soon apparent that this was on a popular bicycle route as fellow cyclists cranked by. A few of them cried out, "Bon jour!" – making me realize how close to Quebec I really was.

Vermonters have a rightful reputation of being independent thinkers. It was many years past the notion of the original 13 colonies that Republic of Vermont allowed itself to become part of the Union as the 14th state in 1791. The one thing Vermonters might agree on is they live in a beautiful place.

I, for one, enjoyed the dips and twists along the shores of Lake Champlain. In 1998, some local politicians deemed this body of water worthy of a Great Lake status. That didn't last long. A few weeks later it went back to being good old Lake Champlain.

The lake was named after Samuel de Champlain, a French explorer, way back in the 1600s. Through the course of history the area was claimed by numerous Native American tribes, the French, the British and now, Vermont. The small northern portion of the lake is owned by Quebec, Canada. It has been a busy lake.

While pedaling securely within the United State, I noticed well-tended organic gardens, clean-cut homes and friendly natives waving sincere hellos from their riding lawnmowers. The pleasant terrain kept my mind and body removed from the fact I wasn't excited about riding 65 miles to Burlington. I was still scorched from going long on the previous day's ride.

I hauled into South Hero, which was actually named for a hero. The stud muffin in question was Revolutionary War star Ethan Allen. History didn't draw me to a halt; it was a bagel shop. While inhaling my second breakfast, I realized that this might have been some of the most memorable scenery of this journey. How could anyone not approve of the views of the mountains and lake?

After my bagel break, I joined the Lake Champlain Bikeway, which led through the suburbs of Burlington past marinas, parks and across the Winooski River. The cycling scene on the trail ranged from determined triathletes to wobbly wheeled adolescents. All groups seemed to be quite content at the progress they were making.

I encountered Don at Burlington's downtown ferry dock. Don is another cycling acquaintance (our mutual friend is Bill Beaster) who was willing to drive five hours from Stamford, Conn., to pay me a visit. He also is retired and has some time of his hands. Personally, I think he wanted to take a long run in his hot new sports car. Whatever the reason, it was good to see him.

Over lunch and brews we played catch up on buddies and travels. Like so many folks I spoke to, Don said, "I'd love to do what you are doing. I just can't seem to pedal more than 40 miles a day."

"Why not have Mary (his wife) follow you in the camper?" I said. "That way you can take 'home' with you."

By the look on his face, I could tell he didn't think much of my suggestion.

We hung around Church Street alternating between coffee and beer breaks. We got an up-close look at the spike-haired, tattooed and fish-hook impaled masses listlessly strolling by.

"Sure is an eclectic group of people in this town," Don said.

We parted ways at sunset for my scheduled visit to get reacquainted with Burlington locals Anne and Andy. During the previous summer, I spent a night with this couple while taking in a Vermont Lake Monsters baseball game. They were another Warm Showers List connection, although they were very different than most. My hosts' bicycle resume included a cross-country ride and a yearlong circumnavigation of our planet. I felt unworthy in their presence.

Anne is an energetic, outgoing and obviously happy human. She moves in various tangents in the physical and mental sense. This is all good. She concludes each thought and sentence with a dazzling smile.

Andy's personality is more along the lines of "slow down and let's think about this." Once again the yin-yang concept of relationships seemed to be at hand and working.

Now they are raising two well-mannered boys, have careers and stay much closer to home. Over dinner, I got the opportunity to see how this adventuresome couple shifted gears to being responsible and caring parents. I felt like an outsider looking in, all too aware this facet of the human experience would always be foreign to me.

In the morning, the parents went off to work, the kids to daycare and me downtown for a day of catching up on chores and R&R.

I was waiting for Sean to show up for his inaugural self-contained bike tour. I've known Sean on and off for more than three decades. I met him back when I worked as a seasonal forester in the Big Horn Mountains of Wyoming. I have a vivid memory of my first observation of Sean. He and a few fellow U.S. Forest Service employees were tongue-kissing a stuffed moose in a bar. I never understood why, although it does get lonely in Wyoming at times.

Now he is a paunchy, middle-aged guy who falls in the weekend-warrior class of athletes. In the times I visited him in his home setting, he was the undisputed ruler of the roost. His persona is larger than his 6-foot frame. I've been with him on enough mini-adventures to know that when he gets tired, he becomes more argumentative, moody and can be a bit of a bully. I try and steer clear of him when that happens.

Sean was scheduled to escort me for a week. I was taking a wait-and-see approach to that. He's a busy guy who flies commercial airplanes for a living. Between work, a wife, three kids, extended family, and friends, his full plate becomes a full trough.

He eventually showed up looking a bit worn out before ever getting on the bike. While we were partaking in Happy Hour, he handled one phone call after another. Life is not easy for a self-appointed "people fixer." I wasn't envious of his acquired position.

Before we departed in the morning, Sean, an ex-Navy pilot, insisted on a pre-ride briefing.

"What if I wipe out and wake up in a ditch? What's the plan?"

"Call 911 like everyone else does. Then, when you have a moment, phone me."

An answer like that really pisses him off.

"Sean! I've been at this game for a long time. Get on your bike, ride and stop in Plainfield. Please don't make this dramatic."

We finally left Burlington on Highway 2 heading east. For a state that ranks 48 out of the 50 in population, the road was crazy busy. The smooth and wide shoulders of New York State had disappeared. We hugged the white line as trucks blew by.

With a slight breeze at our backs we moved adjacent to the Winooski River toward Montpelier. Upon seeing the gold-domed state capitol building from about one mile away, I wondered: How understated can a state capital be? The town felt like "Andy of Mayberry" minus the southern accents and Barney Fife.

En route to Plainfield we passed signs advertising woodcarvers, cheese makers, fresh veggies and psychic readings. The whole area had a New Agey, '70s feel about it. I even noticed a few Jerry Garcia look-alikes. It was a heck of a lot more interesting then gun shops and gas stations.

Upon arrival in Plainfield, we secured our rides to a lamppost and waited to get a call from old friend, Bob. He was a Syracuse acquaintance who lived in the same "Animal House" environment I did in our bomb-proof days. In those wild and crazy years, his nickname was O Bob. The O was short for organic. Way before healthy eating was a desired trait, O Bob was all over it. In our co-op he pushed vegetarian meals to a meat-and-potatoes crowd. He was surely ahead of his time in the mid-1970s.

While loitering around, an attractive hard-bodied woman came by and asked, "Are you waiting for Bob?"

"Yes, we are."

"Bob called and said you would be leaving your bikes at my house. He's on his way."

Word gets around quickly in a small Vermont town.

Sean and I walked over to the food co-op, which was the only market in town. Upon entering, I felt as if we had gone back in time to those tie-dye years of the '70s. We purchased a pound of organic coffee, a few pieces of organic fruit and even a six-pack of organic beer. It was the least I could do after not seeing O Bob since 1976.

O Bob was waiting for us by our bikes. He hadn't changed much. His dodgy old ponytail had gone missing, and that was about it. Other than that, Bob was now married to Beth, had two teenage sons and had become Vermont's state botanists. He always was a positive, good-natured and nurturing sort. That evening during family time, I realized those attributes improved through the years. The aging process did not leave him cynical and jaded. I was impressed.

Once again, I played catch up with an old friend. Once again, I was thrilled he had allowed me back into his life even for just a night.

On a cool morning, Sean insisted upon another briefing. "Sean! Today's mission is to ride 56 miles to Lancaster, New Hampshire. Upon arrival, we will secure food, shelter and beer. Are there any questions?"

"Where do we eat lunch?"

"We can execute a refueling stopover in St. Johnsbury, Vermont. We will then slip across the border to New Hampshire. Will you accept this mission? There will be hills."

He muttered a few choice words at me before heading east on manic Highway 2. It was a stiff climb out of the Winooski River valley and up and over to the Passumpsic River basin, where the quintessential New England town of St. Johnsbury lies.

Sean arrived and dismounted unsteadily. "I'm beat! Those climbs were long."

"We'll get some lunch and move out. We have to cross up and over into the Connecticut River watershed after this."

Between bites of lunch Sean dialed out and received an array of phone calls. It's not easy being a fixer to the world's ills.

After some digesting, we tackled the climbs. Along the ridgelines we were rewarded with views of the nearby White Mountains. It's usually true; the scenery improves with altitude. Maybe that's why I've spent most of my life in Colorado.

At Lunenburg, I turned hard right and dropped off Highway 2 toward the Connecticut River. I wanted to get a look-see at the Mount Olne covered bridge. It's a newish bridge constructed in 1911. The original was taken out by a log-jam in the 1860s or 1870s. I crossed the wooden deck to the eastern side and arrived in New Hampshire. I waited for Sean to show before meandering into Lancaster.

Not Long in New Hampshire

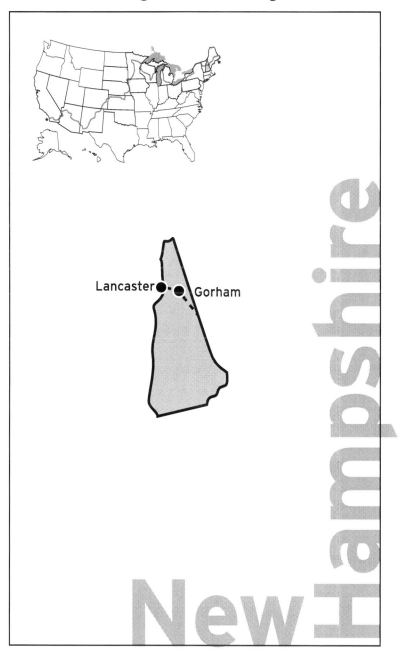

17. Not Long in New Hampshire

"Engine Two! Westside ambulance! Respond to a report of gunfire with possible victims at … Fort Collins PD advises staging a safe distance from the scene. PD will notify you when the scene is secure."

We barreled out of the station with the ambulance close behind and soon were in the general vicinity of the call. Unfortunately, this scene was a work in progress and our position was far from secure.

Just as Roger, our driver, applied the air brakes, the perpetrator stopped in front of the engine and popped off a few rounds at the pursuing police. We all tried to become smaller targets by slinking down low inside the cab. Ron Richardson, a fire department-friendly officer if there ever was one, was in hot pursuit. He used the engine for cover as he replied back with fire power. The only weapons we had were a few axes and spanner wrenches. Amazingly, no stray projectiles ventured our way.

Once the shooter was past us, we went in to survey the carnage. He had killed his mother outright and wounded a neighbor. We loaded the neighbor into the ambulance. She was conscious, orientated and alert. Her gunshot wound was in her thigh. We staunched the blood flow with trauma dressings and got down to business.

She was with the program enough to ask, "Is this ambulance bullet-proof?"

Sean emerged from the Vermont side of the bridge, his legs stained with chain grease. It was a sure sign of a few wobbly dismounts. "I had to get off on a few of those climbs. I'm whooped."

It was a short, flat six miles along the bucolic Connecticut River to Lancaster. We scored a room in a central location, had a few hotel room beers and began the cleaning up process.

Sean was on the phone and allowed me to get first dibs at the bathroom. I did my wash and dry and made an off-hand comment to Sean: "The faucet in the sink just dribbles out water, but the shower is fine." He stumbled in.

That evening, Sean was sliding into grumpy-and-moody mode as a result of the day's exertion. He's one of the few people I know who gets more cantankerous with muscle fatigue. The dinner conversation headed south in a short time. "What did you mean by that?" became his typical response to me.

"Sean! Relax! I meant nothing by that. You're tired. Have another beer and relax."

We got back to the hotel and I read before lights-out time. He took phone calls and watched a TV show eulogizing Sen. Ted Kennedy, who had just passed away. Around 9:30, Sean asked me, "Are you carrying any tools?"

"Yeah, a few basic ones. Is there anything wrong with your bike?"

"No! I can fix that sink faucet with a wrench. Get up and give me the tools."

"Sean, we are not buying the place. We are leaving in 10 hours. There is no need for you to be a fixer here."

Wrong thing for me to say. With that comment, he was off to the races.

"Jeff, that's just like you to ignore the problem and just walk away. That is exactly what my sisters would do" That wasn't meant as a compliment.

There is nothing like an argument before bed to induce a crappy night of sleep. In the morning, we awoke to Tropical Storm Danny, which had washed up on the shores of New Hampshire and beyond. The temperature had plummeted. The wind was an in-your-face easterly and rain pelted down. I looked at Sean and very honestly said, "I'm heading out to Gorham; it's 25 miles away. At this point, I don't care if you come or not. I'm going." I left soon thereafter.

En route, I was supposed to see mountains named after ex-presidents. With the low-level clouds, fog and mist, they remained shrouded in mystery. I made it to Gorham, got a room and left a phone message for Sean. I headed into a wet town for a meal. A five-muffin breakfast doesn't last long on a chilly 25-mile day. I fueled up and returned through the dreary scene. Sean had arrived at the hotel.

"I called my wife. She's coming to get me in a few hours."

Deep down inside, I expelled a sigh of relief. This was no Brad or Calvin or a happy-go-lucky, easy-going dude. This was drama. My inner peace and tranquility would soon be restored. The whole episode reminded me of those sleazy barroom signs: "All our customers make us happy. Some by coming, some by leaving." Take a guess which customer Sean was.

We shook hands, said "Good luck!" and off I went for a quiet dinner and brews.

I slept blissfully that night and discovered the storm had passed with the exodus of Sean. Both events were good. With the glorious weather, I felt invigorated enough to take a side trip to view New Hampshire's highest peak – Mount Washington.

Traffic was as gentle as the uphill grade. I smiled again feeling a renewed sense of freedom.

New Hampshire and freedom go hand and hand: After all, the state's license plate motto is "Live Free or Die." It's a harsh, controversial commentary from the hard-nosed denizens of the Granite State. Personally, I would be more inclined to the motto, "Live Free or Let's Talk About Other Options Over a Beer."

At Pinkham Notch, I caught a glimpse of Mount Washington through the clouds. This summit is nothing to be trifled with. At 6,288 feet, it stands above all the rest in the northeast. It's also the world record holder for the highest wind gust ever measured – 231 mph.

I would not advise trying to ride a bicycle in those conditions. The mountain also has a justifiable and nasty reputation for killing the unprepared.

Darby Field pulled off the first recorded ascent of the mountain by a white guy in 1642. That effort must have worn him out, as he died at the age of 39. His epic journey took him a walloping 18 days to execute. Now that is perseverance.

It was a downhill run along the Ellis River to Conway. On that Sunday, the coffee houses, outdoor cafés and knick-knack shops were going full bore. I threaded my way through town, avoiding aggressive bargain hunters in SUVs and Subarus.

A few miles later, I stopped on a bridge overlooking the Saco River. Below me colorful watercrafts bobbed by. I had entered Maine, the 17th and final state of my cross-country ride.

Mighty Amazed to Be in Maine

18. Mighty Amazed to be in Maine

Jane, my girlfriend at the time, and I were dropping off a vehicle for repairs en route to our jobs. I went into the office to leave the keys and do the paperwork for the hurtin' unit and Jane stayed with the other car. While I was taking care of business, she was doing her usual rocking out listening to the radio.

When I got back to the car, Jane cried out, "A plane flew into the World Trade Center! It just came over the radio!"

Without a moment's hesitation I said one word: "Terrorists." It was Sept. 11, 2001.

I dropped off Jane at her office and hustled over to Fire Station 10. The three crew members of B shift sat mesmerized as the TV screen showed both towers spewing smoke. One minute before my shift officially began, the South Tower collapsed. The rest is history and our world hasn't been the same.

The shift was a quiet one, as if accidents, sickness and fires decided to pay homage to the deceased and tread lightly. Our chiefs made a few conference calls to the crews in an awkward attempt to fill in the gaps. It seemed to me they, too, were at a loss for words. But then again, how can anyone explain the inexplicable?

At the time I resided near Old Town in Fort Collins. It's the showcase of the city and the place to see and be seen. For many days and nights after the tragedy, the area's usual revelry and high energy were missing. The downtown scene had a muted, library-like tone. I half expected someone to say, "Shhhhh …" if anyone got too loud. I assumed most folks were hunkered down with family, friends and significant others. The term "cocooning" became very popular.

Another spin-off of 911, both locally and on a national level, was America's rediscovery of emergency service workers. Almost overnight, firefighters became the nation's heroes.

Many of my comrades jumped onto the bandwagon by purchasing designer license plates announcing to the world they were a "Firefighter." More than a few began wearing their "Fire Dept." T-shirts off-duty. I felt uncomfortable in that role. When people asked me what I did for a living, I'd respond, "I work for the city."

As an ex-New Yorker and a firefighter, the events of 911 certainly hit a nerve with me. Like proverbial moths to flame; firefighters move toward burning buildings. We are trained and get paid to take chances to save people and property. That, in a nutshell, is what we do.

The 343 New York firefighters and paramedics who died in the ultimate performance of duty that day were caught in the "fog of war" called structural firefighting.

Many years before the world ever heard of al Qaeda and the Taliban, I visited a friend of a friend in the South Tower. He was working in a cubicle on the 89th floor. I said hello and made a remark about his panoramic view of the New York harbor.

"Yeah, I get paid a crappy salary, but I have a million dollar view!" he said.

I still wonder if he was working in the tower on 9-11 and whether he made it out alive.

I took a photo of an extremely understated "Welcome" sign. It simply read, "Maine State Line." Then again, the citizens of the "Vacationland" state have never been known to be overly demonstrative. The highway was a hodgepodge of cracks, potholes and just plain dirt. I guided my front wheel through the obstacle course as best as I could. Maybe the state motto should be changed to, "Our scenery makes up for our crummy infrastructure."

The look of Maine was feral, boggy, primitive and overgrown. I liked that. It had been 30 years since I last pedaled in this northeast outpost of America. Where did all the cars and trucks come from? No matter: The crazy green landscape made up for the scary roads and drivers.

I called it a night in Bridgton. I walked into town from my on-the-outskirts hotel and noticed a lamp and doll repair shop. It was a different sort of cottage industry than I saw in Vermont. This was more practical and less New-Agey. It seemed appropriate to Maine.

While at another barroom feed, I reached out to a long distance friend via my cell phone. Kathy is a Colorado buddy who knows the real me. She made this astute observation: "Jeff! You don't want this ride to end, do you?" She had a point there.

Good thing I had a few bonus miles up my sleeve and a hike to the tallest mountain in Maine to prolong the inevitable.

It was an undulating ride toward Norway (the town, not the country) where I was to have my first encounter with Robin and her mom, Jean. I met Robin on an Internet dating site called "Plenty of Fish." I suppose it's based on the premise that there are plenty of fish in the sea. Let me tell you as a professional single guy, I would have to agree with the world's fisheries experts: The seas are getting depleted.

Nevertheless, Robin turned out to be a vivacious, smiling, creative and energetic woman. Her quiet mom was sweet, too.

Robin lived in Tucson, Ariz., a place I was about to move to. We had been "chatting" on the Internet for a few weeks. She happened to be visiting her old hometown in New Hampshire at the same time I was in the New England. She was en route to see her brother in northern Maine, and our paths crossed in Norway at the Nomad Coffeehouse.

Through this convoluted process, we met for the first time, face to face. This was a far cry from the dating practices of my parent's generation. Over coffee and scones we worked out some family history, a few likes and dislikes and a tale or three. This was speed dating to the extreme.

We were similar ages but have taken divergent paths in our lives. Robin chose many of the clichés the Baby Boom generation was known for: the back-to-nature movement, communes and now a New-Age church. She found time to raise two children and get divorced twice. She seemed happy to be living within the oasis she created for herself in Tucson. Who am I to judge another's path to nirvana?

After a few photo ops (Jean did not like to have her picture taken), they returned to their sedan for five more hours of driving northward.

I hopped back on my bike with the added weight of a wild turkey feather Robin bestowed upon me.

She gave me a warm hug and said, "Call me when you get to Tucson."

I did that eventually. I think she liked my bike.

From Norway, my route took me past Paris (the village not the city) and into summer. From the evidence of uprooted trees, toppled-over sheds and missing roof shingles, a wind-borne calamity had recently struck there. It might not have been a 231-mph gust, but for the locals, it must have felt that way.

Continuing to Hartford and Canton, I noticed 24-7 garage sales of used and rusted appliances spilling out onto the right of way. Their owners sat nearby smoking cigarettes. By their disbelieving looks, I'm pretty certain I was off-route for most of Maine's touring cyclists.

I noticed property lines delineated by boulders or rubble. This must have been a modern Maine version of Fred Flintstone's town of Bedrock. It all seemed so appropriate.

At the Androscoggin River, logging trucks became plentiful on the shoulder-less, pitted road. For the drivers, making time was equivalent to making money. I would hear the brutes approaching and timidly peel off into the dirt. Yes, I was scared of them.

The traffic in to Farmington was like something you would expect in Mexico City. I managed to survive a four-lane highway crossing to a hotel. While checking in I asked the clerk, "What's up with all this traffic?"

In that unmistakable "Down East" accent he drawled an answer: "Well, the railroad stopped moving freight so there are more trucks on the road. A big shoe factory closed down nearby, so folks have to commute farther for work. If that's not bad enough, there are a wicked number of roads converging in Farmington."

An explanation clear and concise – just what you'd expect from a Mainer.

I checked my email while relaxing in my room. One subject line got my immediate attention: "Iowa Cyclist Killed by Hit and Run Driver." In this no-nonsense manner, I heard the horrific news about a biker buddy, Mark. He was an all-around nice guy, gentleman and artist, a jeweler by trade. I fondly remembered Mark as the guy being on the edge of the party on the GRABAAWR. You would look his way and see him smile. He would give you a reassuring thumb's up. His low-key approach to being classy was a trait many could learn from.

His life was snuffed out in Des Moines by a reckless pickup truck driver. He was 54 years old. It was a violent death; poor Mark was thrown 130 feet and died at the scene. At the time of the email posting, the police were still looking for the scumbag who took his life. Mark's family and friends were searching for an answer to how this could have happened to such a good human being. Can anyone really find an answer?

A few days later, the hit-and-run driver was apprehended by the police. He was caught trying to pull an incriminating dent out of his truck. No wonder I had the heebie-jeebies while riding that day.

I rolled three miles into town for a meal at a brewpub that wasn't. "We used to make our own beer," the bartender said. "But to be honest, our beer was lousy."

The nice bartender told me about the Farmington Prophecy. The idea was floated by a Quaker named Licia Kuenning, who spoke about a "coming new order." On June 6, 2006, (666) the town was supposed to undergo a wonderful transformation. There would be no more deaths, illnesses, crime or poor behavior after that date. There was one catch: No one could venture outside the town's limits to obtain these gifts. Even in the world of prophecies, there is fine print. When 666 came and went and nothing happened, the event was rescheduled "within the next few years." It's a fine prophecy for a mid-sized college town. As of yet, I have not purchased property in Farmington.

I chowed down and headed back up Highway 2 before the sunset since I wanted to be seen by all drivers. That night my sleep was in bits and pieces: I might have been thinking about Mark.

I woke to Sept. 1 and a true feeling of autumn. The air had a clean, cool freshness about it, just like a Canadian beer in the gaseous state. Yellow school buses performed their tasks of picking up tykes. I was into the fifth month of my journey and had seen two seasons come and go. Where did those months and seasons go? Maybe time does fly when you are having fun.

I took breakfast at the Farmington Truck Stop, figuring if it was good enough for log-truck drivers, it was good enough for me. While paying my bill, I asked Suzie if she was familiar with the local roads.

"Yep! Born and raised here. Wad'ya needs to know?"

I told her I was in the mood for quiet roads to get to Bingham. I was feeling vulnerable and exposed after learning of Mark's demise.

"That'll be 43, then 148, then 16."

I flew by towns that had gone missing from Maine's AAA map. On a stretch of road a few miles from Farmington, a sign announced I was in Industry. There was none and not much evidence of people, either. Perfect.

Past Allens Mills, I chanced upon a one-man logging operation. An old-time logger complete with flannel shirt and hardhat was taking his lunch break. His wife had brought him his roadside nourishment.

"I get the feeling you've been in this line of work for some time," I said.

"Yep! For a few years," he said in classic Maine understatement.

I didn't find out the exact number of years his faithful wife brought him lunch while he went about his business of cutting eastern white pines.

After arriving in Bingham for the night, I set off for Thompson's restaurant for another breakfast/lunch. I asked the waitress what was the driving force behind the town.

"We used to have a few sawmills here. Now, for some reason, the logs are heading north to Canada."

That seemed odd. I was near U.S. Route 201, also known as the old Canada Road, which served as a major link between Maine and Quebec from 1820 to 1860. Apparently, the U.S. logging industry had rediscovered the route.

Bingham, population 1,000, had seen better days. The lone pub in town was boarded up – never a positive sign in a blue-collar town with an excess of winter.

I got a room and walked across the road while dodging logging trucks. I sat on the banks of the Kennebec River, popped open a tall-boy Budweiser and enjoyed my solitary Happy Hour as the river toppled along. On that sunny shore, all I could was think, "this is living."

When the sun went down I ambled over to a truck stop for dinner. At 7 p.m. it was the only place open in Bingham. A local character named Russell was providing mealtime entertainment. He sang, recited poetry and told jokes, all in a loud voice. The laid-back Mainers just went along with it. Every so often, one would pipe up and say, "Yup!"

Russell looked the part of a true Down Easterner. He wore high-water wool trousers, a button-down collar flannel shirt and long white socks into which he tucked his trousers. He even provided up-to-the minute weather reports: "It's 75 degrees now. It's so hot!"

A few replied, "Yup!"

I grabbed another beer and a pizza and retired to my loft apartment across the street. Sleep came easy along the Kennebec.

I woke before dawn and trudged back to the truck stop for breakfast. Coffee was free after I ordered the Hungry Logger's Special. Such a deal!

I was fortified for my slog out of the Kennebec River Valley. The grades were Tour de France steep, the road's surface a patchwork of asphalt. Of course, there were logging trucks. I started to suspect

Maine's soccer moms used these behemoth vehicles for the simple task of dropping off little Johnny at school. Sedans were certainly the exception in rural Maine. Yup!

I huffed and puffed for miles out of the rushing river valley. At the road's crest, a sign on the opposite side of the road stated: "Warning! Steep downhill for 4 miles." It wasn't me being a weenie – it was freaking steep.

I rolled through Guilford and Dover-Foxcroft enjoying the roadside attraction of the Piscataquis River. For a guy like me from the high-desert mountain state of Colorado, all this fluid was hard to fathom. I loved it.

I made it into Milo for a two-night stopover. The plan was to pay a long overdue visit to Sheilah, Jensen and Mount Katahdin. Twenty-three years had gone by since I last saw the three. Considering how I felt about these friends and mountain, that was too long.

Sheilah and Jensen are former forestry college chums who met in school and married. In this remote Maine outpost, they managed to raise two sons.

Since my last visit, Jensen had been promoted to the auspicious title of director of Maine's largest state park – Baxter. In California, this would be the equivalent of head honcho in Yosemite National Park. This was an impressive accomplishment for my serious, earnest and capable friend. But don't let that focused approach to reality fool you. Every now and then, Jensen will spout out a hilarious mini-burst of irony, leaving one to exclaim, "Where did that line come from?"

Sheilah, on the other hand, took a Jim Carrey approach to life. She's out there – in a good way. She is quick with a jibe followed closely by a mischievous twinkle in her eye. While we attended school, her nickname was the "Dairy Queen" for her wholesome good looks and page-boy hairstyle. In a college where men outnumbered women four to one, she stood out as a certifiable babe.

For me, it was pure joy to be back in their company again.

As far as Mount Katahdin went, how often does one have the opportunity to climb Maine's highest peak with the director of Baxter?

My hosts rolled in from work as another round of hugs and handshakes were doled out. It was time once again to play catch up with old friends. While we ate a carbo-loaded dinner of baked ziti, the cool couple provided a dialogue on the usual topics of family, work and our aging process. We called it an early night to catch some Z's for our 4:30 a.m. wake up call for Katahdin.

En route to Baxter, Jensen explained the history of this unique park. I sipped coffee and asked lots of questions. It was like having my own private visitor center. Jensen was able to recite names, dates and local lore with Google-like quickness. He pulled this off without the benefit of a coffee fix. I tried absorbing as many Baxter factoids as my early-morning brain would allow.

The park was a big green-and-granite gift to the people of Maine from Gov. Percival P. Baxter. He had a knack for schmoozing and negotiating with landowners. He also had a personal bank roll to help seal the deal. This was no overnight land grab. It took the patient governor 32 years to purchase and donate more than 200,000 acres to the Pine Tree State.

Jensen had a pre-dawn meeting to attend before we began our climb. I watched as he interacted with park visitors and staff. For this director, there was no such thing as being "off duty." Governor Baxter can rest in peace knowing his park is in good hands.

Jensen finagled a way for us to do an up-and-over traverse of Mount Katahdin, which is also known as Baxter Peak. From start to the finish we were afforded new views at every turn. Unfortunately, there weren't many turns. Apparently in the early days of trail building, the shortest distance between two points was the way to go. There wasn't even a rumor of a switchback. I needed to lunge and pull myself over boulders as I utilized a set of leg muscles that had lain dormant on the bike. After all, I had just been sitting on my butt for the past 17 weeks. The only walking I had done was to the bars and back to my hotel. Those ambles were usually flat and required little gymnastic skills.

By Colorado standards, a peak a shade over a mile high (5,268 feet) would be considered a bad joke. In these almost-in-Canada northern climes, the summit is above tree line. This was no Mount Sunflower (Kansas) or Hawkeye Point (Iowa) high point: This was a real and gasp-inducing mountain.

Once we gained the top, I watched my friend shift into his official role as he answered questions and handed out useful info to a few park guests. I didn't mind; it gave me an opportunity to don three more layers of fleece and snap a few panoramic photos. I had to pinch myself to stop from thinking, "I'm back in the Rockies." It was a stellar moment of my journey.

Katahdin is doubly famous as being the northern terminus for the 2,181-mile Appalachian Trail. Beginning in Georgia, the AT is a long-distance hike embedded within the soul of America's notion of the Great Outdoors. At the Mount Katahdin sign, two young, bearded and trail-hardened hikers had just completed a five-month adventure. They were all hair and grins as they had their photos taken. I wondered if behind those smirks they were thinking about what the end of their journey meant. Could it be a sad, "What now?" That's a question I would soon be asking myself.

Jensen and I struck poses as others snapped our photo. We then began our descent through clammy, wispy clouds. As I took a last downward glance at Maine, I knew it was all descent to the Atlantic Ocean from here.

We hustled down past a few clueless hikers wearing flip-flops, dress shoes and Aqua Socks. We just shook our heads while thinking they were disasters waiting to happen. By the time we made it back to the truck, I was hobbling. I was in need of food, beer and a handful of aspirins, and not necessarily in that order. I wondered if Mount Katahdin had grown or gotten steeper since my last summit 23 years ago. I hate to think the problem was me getting older and slower.

Sweetheart Sheilah had a surprise for us – Maine lobsta! Their son, Noah, drove up from the University of Maine/Farmington to join in the get-together. When I met the lad, I announced, "Noah! You weren't even a rumor the last time I was here." The family got a chuckle out of that.

Noah was a chip off the old block with his positive approach to life and look-you-in-the-eye personality. It didn't take long for me to realize this was one well-mannered, intelligent and interesting young man. His proud parents watched as Noah and I bantered back and forth, obviously enjoying our show.

After the Maine lobsta, potatoes, corn, melted butter and four brews, I slowly climbed upstairs to bed.

I woke sore and still worn out at 5 a.m., but I wanted to say goodbye and thanks to Baxter's boss. I told Jensen that my day's destination would be Lincoln. He gave it some thought and exclaimed, "You will soon understand its nickname – Stinking Lincoln." He made it sound so appealing. For me, the appeal was the short distance; only 35 miles away on shaky legs. I liked that despite the threat of a paper-mill stench.

We shook hands and agreed 23 years was too long without a visit. He asked me, "Would you consider a canoe or backpack trip in the northeast in a few years?"

My smile and enthusiastic nod told him the answer.

Sheilah rolled out of bed shortly after. We were soon laughing over yarns past and present.

"We plan on being in Florida in April. Want to visit us? Jensen and you can go see the Tampa Bay Rays play."

Now that's an offer I will find hard to refuse. I caught a hug and was off for my final run to Bar Harbor. As usual, I would be traveling in a convoluted manner to get there.

From Milo, I turned onto a dirt road and left my worries (logging trucks) behind. In the parlance of cyclists, this was a "good" dirt road. The definition being a skinny-tired bike wouldn't get mired in the gravel and grit. The weather cooperated with a blazing skin-warming sun and a gentle tailwind.

It was the start of the Labor Day weekend. I had been on the road through all the benchmarks of summer – Memorial Day, Fourth of July and now Labor Day. I'd been at this game for some time. I didn't need a weatherman to tell me the obvious. Signs were all about: maple tree leaves turning crimson, piles of firewood stacked like mini-forts in front of homes and Labor Day sales for snow blowers.

The time had come to put a fork in this ride and call it done.

At a gentle bend in the road, two Mainers watched as I negotiated the dirt. One called out, "Must get good gas mileage on that thing."

"Not really! I make up for it with all the food I eat."

From there we went through the Q&A period of bicycle touring. "San Diego? You're joking. Right?"

"Nope! Today's a short day; just 35 miles to Lincoln."

"That's short to you?"

"It's all relative."

They gave me the two-thumbs up sign and wished me a safe journey.

I crossed a few large rivers and caught a whiff of a pulp mill every now and then. It was early when I arrived at a Lincoln hotel. As fatigued as I felt, I didn't mind. I napped, swallowed a few aspirin for my achy legs and went back to bed early. No one would ever be envious of my wild-and-crazy night life when on the road.

While I slept, the stinking-Lincoln syndrome began. Either the mill ramped up production when the sun sank low or the wind shifted. Even my dreams stank.

I knew it was going to be a long day as I followed Highway 6 mostly uphill. My legs still felt wobbly from the Katahdin climb. The scenery continued to be trees, more trees, a few bogs and a hefty lake thrown into the mix for good measure. The views weren't eye-catching, but at least the traffic was mellow. In the jargon of cyclists, this was a travel day.

I ran into U.S. 1 at Topsail and followed it south. This old highway (1920s) runs along the east coast from the Canadian border all the way to Margaritaville, also known as Key West, Fla. While it merrily goes along its 2,377 miles, the meandering route bisects many of America's largest cities.

While growing up in the Bronx, I and a few other young explorers would ride U.S. 1 north to New Rochelle. We imagined seeing more blond-haired girls there. For a bunch of snot-nosed kids, this was a true adventure. Apparently, I enjoyed the feel of seeing what's out there. I was still at it decades later.

Past Princeton lays the Moosehorn National Wildlife Refuge. Not only is this the easternmost bird hangout on the Atlantic flyway, it's one of the oldest, dating back to 1937. The day I was there, I saw more birders bearing binoculars than birds.

Calais is a border town with St. Stephen, New Brunswick, Canada. Once again, Old Glory shared airspace with the Maple Leaf flag of our northern neighbor. In the grocery stores, Budweiser sat longneck-to-longneck with Labatt, and Canadian coinage mixed freely with its American counterparts. I slept that night in the International Hotel.

The natural border between the two countries is the St. Croix River. Its water is brackish, influenced by the ebb and flow of the ocean's tides. I knew then my journey was in its closing stages.

At the pub where I took my Happy Hour and dinner, the bartender informed me, "There will be a band here tonight for the long weekend. You should stick around."

I looked at my watch and chuckled. Me? Stay up late? Yeah, right. It would take more than a garage band to keep this worn out rider from his 9:30ish beddy-bye time.

As luck would have it, an autumn high pressure system was holding for my ride to Machias. I turned off U.S. 1 at an official National Park Service sign announcing the St. Croix International Historical Site. Here I discovered the failed French settlement on St. Croix Island. While I read the informational placards amid the larger-than-life bronze statues of Passamaquoddy tribesmen, French craftsmen and soldiers, a familiar name popped up. In 1604, good old Samuel de Champlain, mapmaker and explorer, was present and accounted for. He later set out farther north and west and founded Quebec City in 1608. He was in search of the elusive Northwest Passage to the Orient but land kept getting in his way.

In Perry, a square road marker demarcated the line of the 45th parallel. My bicycle straddled the halfway point between the equator and the North Pole. Placards explained how the early surveyors came to this conclusion. While I looked at the grainy black-and-white photos of those hardworking perfectionists, I realized riding a bicycle was an easier task. Maybe it was just my imagination, but it seemed warmer on the south side of the marker.

I yearned to see the Atlantic Ocean and was willing to ride bonus miles to accomplish that. I veered off at Whiting in order to visit Lubec and Quoddy Head State Park. Both are famous as being the easternmost something in the United States – Lubec is the town; Quoddy Head State Park is the extreme eastern point. Hey! Why not?

I'll tell you why not. Maine's roads are four-wheel drive rough and hilly, and to be frank, I was tired! The closest I got was seeing the easternmost sign for the town of Lubec. After consulting my map, watch and noticing my fatigued state, this was as close as I would get.

I cut my losses and turned on Highway 191. The road had some rollers to deal with, but at least the pavement was good. My sore bottom was thankful for that. At Cutler, the Atlantic Ocean came in view. Lobster boats bobbed in the bay as multi-colored traps dried upon the shore. I had arrived at the Atlantic Ocean, but I wasn't quite done.

Back on U.S. 1, signs proclaimed this segment as the "Coastal Road." From this humble bicycle rider's point of view, that was false advertising. The only waves in sight were the numerous crests and troughs of the road. This torturous cycling landscape was a result of ancient glaciers carving a southern route to the sea. My shell-shocked legs wished for a wide, flat, river delta instead.

After 78 miles and seven hours, I arrived in Machias. I suffered an instant insult to injury when I was informed by the hotel clerk the town's only pub (the Thirsty Moose) was closed on Sundays. It's a grand thing gas stations sell beer on the Lord's Day.

My hotel sided up to the Machias River, which is another brackish stream. While lovey-dovey couples sipped wine in the waning sunlight, I watched cormorants dive for their dinners. For me, this was a pretty entertaining Happy Hour show.

I woke to a gauzy sky and wired myself with another round of caffeine. That invincible energy lasted until Jonesboro. In Columbia Falls, I was drawn off U.S. 1 by a giant blueberry, or at least a building that looked like one. The proprietors were in the business of selling wild blueberries. It didn't matter if you wanted frozen, fresh or baked, they sold them. I was wearing my cycling jacket to ward off the ocean's chill. One of the blueberry pushers questioned me, "Isn't it nippy for a motorcycle ride?"

"Motorcycle? I'm on a bicycle!"

I said this as I gazed at all the blueberry baked goods. I wasn't noticing the object of my desire. "Do you have any blueberry muffins?"

After hearing that my ride was almost done, she said, "Here's a muffin on us. That way you will remember this place."

I thanked her whole-heartedly for the generous offer. In reality, who could ever forget a structure resembling a giant blueberry?

I eventually peeled off U.S. 1 and onto the rough-and-tumble but wonderfully quiet Mud Creek Road. But that idyllic feeling only lasted for a few miles before entering Highway 3, the gateway road to Bar Harbor and Acadia National Park. Instead of a mellow amble toward my ultimate goal, I dodged vacationers and impatient dump truck drivers.

I gritted my teeth as I avoided wheel-crushing chuckholes. I kept thinking, "How anticlimactic is this?" I crossed over a causeway linking the mainland with Mount Desert Island. The road degenerated even more.

Once in Bar Harbor, I found my bearings and turned onto Cottage Street.

"That's quite a load you are hauling," said a curious bystander.

"Yeah! But I am done!"

"Where did you start?"

"San Diego – about four and a half months ago."

"Congratulations! You must be proud of yourself."

"Not really. I need to down a beer just to settle my nerves. My official ending will be tomorrow when I ride a victory lap in Acadia National Park."

After purchasing a few bottles of Maine beer, I checked into the Cadillac Motel, which would be home for three whole nights of snoozing in the same bed and staying in the same place, a foreign concept for me after all those months.

I popped a top, sat down on the bed and let out a sigh. Other than one small task to perform, I had arrived. To say that I felt worn out would have been an understatement.

That evening after dining on a lobster roll, I explored the bars in Bar Harbor. Why else would they have named a village that? Actually, Bar Harbor's and Acadia National Park's history are closely entwined.

That old French explorer Champlain left his mark here as well. He named the largest island off the coast of Maine, Mount Desert, to describe its barren and treeless peaks. Centuries later, the island was populated by a virtual who's who of America's wealthy families; Pulitzer, Whitney, Rockefeller and Vanderbilt were a few notables who owned super-sized cottages on the island. Luckily for the rest of us, those fabulously rich folks cherished the island so much they donated acreage to the National Park Service. Now Acadia is preserved as a coastal treasure for all with a park pass to enjoy.

I woke with the knowledge that I might have visited one too many bars in Bar Harbor. I moseyed into a café and rejuvenated myself with coffee and another veggie omelet. That morning task completed, I began the final mission of my tour.

From Bar Harbor I found Schooner Head Road and took it into Acadia National Park proper. Not many miles later on a one-way road, I turned toward Sand Beach. There were only a handful of visitors strolling along this small spit of sand. A few brave (maybe simpleminded?) folks submerged themselves in the 55-degree salt water. The Atlantic was calm and tranquil. I pushed and carried my companion to the shore. A cute couple from the Midwest was walking by.

"Excuse me! Would you be kind enough to take my picture? I am done with my cross-country ride," I said.

"Really? We would be happy to."

I pulled out the vial of Pacific Ocean water and upturned it into the Atlantic. There were no obvious repercussions from the blending of the two bodies of water. The woman segment of the nice couple shot the photo. I thanked them. They resumed their morning march as I checked the photo on my digital camera. Unfortunately, she was no Ansel Adams.

I poured some of my water bottle contents into the vial. Another couple came by. "Excuse me …" the drill began again. This time the result was worthy of a finish line photo. I figured if the famous raising of the flag on Iwo Jima was a second take, why couldn't mine be?

It would be a lie to say I was ecstatic about my journey's end. I was already thinking seriously about another cross-country transit from Seattle to Key West.

There were still a few more demons of mine to destroy.

EPILOGUE

I arrived back to my new home in Tucson to empty cupboards after an exploratory trip to St. John, U.S. Virgin Islands. This condition would not do. Despite being whipped from 10 hours of flight time, I decided to head to the local *bodega* for a few essentials. I walked outside in shorts and sweatshirt on a moonless late February evening. It was wilderness-area dark. Tucson is not known for an overabundance of street lights.

I turned a corner onto a busy street and heard a thump followed by the acceleration of a vehicle. A moment later, an old Ford pickup truck blazed by me. I didn't give it much thought until I crossed the busy street and saw a prone man in the headlights of a stopped sedan. There was a young woman wailing over the prostrate body. A Good Samaritan was blocking traffic and speaking on a cell phone. I looked both ways and headed over to see if I could help.

I did a visual once-over of the young man and knew this was a bad situation. Blood was flowing from his nose and ears. His breathing was classic Cheyne-Stokes, as in alternating between deep and shallow breaths. His face was swollen and deformed. Two of his extremities were twisted at odd angles. His carotid pulse was barely palpable.

I spoke to the traffic-control civilian who was still on the phone with 911. "Please pass me the phone as soon as you are able."

He handed it to me right away.

"Dispatch! My name is Jeff; I am a retired firefighter and EMT. Please inform the incoming units this will be a load-and-go situation. The patient has an apparent head injury and possible fractures in his extremities. It might be appropriate to activate a trauma team at the ER, although by the look of the patient it is probably too late for that. By the way, the apparent hit-and-run driver was in an old pickup truck. I saw him heading south on Park Avenue."

It was time to care for the definite living. I leaned over and gently asked the weeping woman, who was the victim's girlfriend, her name.

Between her sobs, she blurted out, "Maria."

"Maria, please come with me. Do you hear those sirens? They are coming to help your boyfriend. You and I must give them room to do their job. They will be moving quickly and you don't want to be in their way. Try to remember all the details of what happened. The police will be asking you lots of questions. The more they know the better the chances of arresting the guy who did this."

The fire department and paramedics arrived about the same time. I tried to pass along patient information, but they were too busy to listen. I steered Maria toward the first policeman on scene. I waited my turn for another patrolman to show up and told him what I saw.

When I looked back, the emergency responders were performing CPR on the victim. After I gave my witness statement, I picked up my shopping bags and continued on to the *bodega*.

Emergency responders leave the job, but the job never leaves them.

I loitered in Acadia National Park and Bar Harbor for some carefree living. After getting my fair share of coastal hiking, lobster rolls and celebratory beers, I boarded a plane from Bangor to New York City. My metal companion would be waiting for me in Colorado. I shipped it home via FedEx.

My brother, Mike, picked me up at LaGuardia Airport. I was looking forward to some family time and a Yankees game.

After a quick hug I got into his car bearing two of my panniers. The police hustled us out of the waiting area. Yes, this was the infamous New York nanosecond in real time.

We were heading east toward the wilds of Long Island when Mike pulled off the highway into a residential neighborhood. He pulled over and stopped the car.

"Mike! What are you doing?"

"I wanted to take a good look at you."

He gave me the head-to-toe, up-and-down look and smiled at me.

"My little brother just rode a bicycle across the country. Isn't that something? I am very proud of you."

For me, that was the best part of my journey.

SORE BOTTOM LINE

- 6,518 miles

- My wheels made contact with 17 states and 15 ballparks.

- What a way to spend 17 weeks, five days. My steed insisted on a respite from the road from time to time. In total, there were two weeks of non-cycling days.

- The machine went through five tires, one set of brakes, a cable, and a soft, cushy seat. The bike held up better than the rider, although it, too, was creaking toward the end.

- I ate enough bananas to satisfy the appetites of all the chimpanzees in Africa. (Looking at something yellow makes me want to peel it.)

- In my wake, there will be an orchard of peaches and nectarines bearing fruit within a few years. Think Johnny Appleseed on a bike.

- I drank the equivalent of Lake Erie in water, beer and coffee. (That is the order of intake, as well.) The saying, "The whole world is a bathroom when you are a guy," is true.

- We live in a beautiful country where most people will just ignore you or be nice to you.

- Go out there and see it before you are so old that walking the pug dog is the highlight of the day.

A SECOND CHANCE

Late lunch? Bonus miles in Glacier National Park? Early Happy Hour?

These were some of my random thoughts as I huffed up the final pull toward the summit of Marias Pass. I was en route from West Glacier, Mont., to East Glacier on what was supposed to be a mellow seven-to-10-day circumnavigation of the Glacier/Waterton National Park complex. I was a mere half hour from completing these decisions when I was thrust into a cave.

Total darkness … no sound … no brakes screeching … no thud of my body smashing the sedan's windshield … no noise as I went rolling and tumbling across 25 feet of asphalt and gravel. When I awoke in a ditch, a Good Samaritan was applying spinal traction to my neck. The peripheral vision from my left eye saw the drip, drip, drip of blood oozing from my nose. My right eye was swollen shut.

"What happened?" I asked weakly.

"You got rear-ended by a car. Don't move!" she answered. She then called out, "He's coming around. I'll need some help here."

I estimated I had checked out of planet Earth for two to four minutes. First responders in civilian clothes assisted me as they poked and prodded my body and took primary and secondary surveys of my injuries.

"Can you move your feet? Can you wiggle them? Squeeze my hands. Are you having trouble breathing?"

The questions came fast and furious: I passed the tests with flying colors. My spinal column was not severed. I was alert enough to pick up a distinct British accent from the crowd gathering above me. I got his attention.

"Was it you who hit me?"

"Yes. I was sightseeing and looking at the mountains and drifted into you."

I might have said a few choice words to him, but I don't recall. I don't remember much, although I remember he never said he was sorry.

An ambulance from Browning arrived and I was placed on an unforgiving backboard and cervical collar. We raced back to the ER with the emergency lights on and sirens blaring. It was a bumpy, rough ride as we careened down the pass and through a construction zone. A paramedic attempted two sticks to get an IV into me and failed both times.

"Please don't stick me again. I hurt enough already. They can do that in the ER under better conditions. I promise I won't die before then."

"OK. We can hold off on it."

"Thanks."

At the ER, a doctor made her orders known: "He'll need a CAT scan of his head. Get a set of X-rays for his neck and spine. Set him up with an IV ASAP. We'll need to monitor his vital signs."

The nurses and technicians efficiently carried out her orders. I was then in the hurry-up-and-wait mode of emergency medicine. A nursing student gently dabbed grit, grime and dried blood from my many facial wounds and multiple areas of road rash. I even had road rash on the tops of my feet. Apparently, the force of the impact literally knocked me out of my shoes.

The compassionate ER doctor came to my side to survey the carnage to my face. She held my hand as she said, "Those lacerations and avulsions will need the care of a plastic surgeon. I can stitch them for you, but they can do a better job. Would you like me to arrange a helicopter transport to Kalispell Regional Medical Center? We can have a plastic surgeon waiting for you."

"Please do. I am not a handsome man to begin with and I can use all the help I can get." With that sad news, I knew my Hollywood contract as George Clooney's double would surely be terminated. Shucks!

"We'll arrange it. The CAT scan of your head and brain came out with negative findings. That is a good thing. We are waiting now for the radiologist to evaluate your neck and spine X-rays."

"Thanks for all the help. Can I get off of this backboard? It is really beginning to hurt me. I'm OK. I can move all of my parts."

"Please wait a few minutes until we get the radiologist report. This is all precautionary."

"OK. I'll try." The pressure point where my head contacted the backboard was starting to throb.

A few minutes (which seemed much longer) later, the nice ER doctor came back. Once again she held my hand.

"I have bad news. The radiologist found 11 fractures in your first 11 vertebrae. You have a broken sternum, too. There will be a neurosurgeon waiting for you in Kalispell, also."

"What? How can that be? I can move all of my parts. Are you sure those were my X-rays?"

"Yes, those were your X-rays. You will get the best of care in Kalispell. I have a special place in my heart for bicycle riders. My son was killed by a driver 20 years ago when he was riding a bike. We will take care of you."

No wonder she was holding my hand.

The helicopter flight crew came and checked me out. "We will hold off on the morphine drip until we get him to Kalispell. Jeff, we are going to give you a scenic ride over Glacier National Park. I am sorry to say you won't get a chance to enjoy the views."

With little fanfare, I was loaded and airborne. They had placed painkillers in my IV, so I became groggy, blurry and disconnected. I remember peeking at the snowcapped mountains briefly. Alas, I would not get to enjoy my $11,000 taxi ride to Kalispell. This was all business.

Upon arrival at my second ER of the day, a plastic surgeon went to work on my tenderized face.

"I will try to stitch you to minimize the scarring. However, there will be some scarring no matter what." All in all, 20 stitches were applied to my eyebrows and right cheek. When she was done she asked. "Would you like to see my work in a mirror?"

"Sure!" I steadied myself for the view. OMG! I was staring at a mini-version of Frankenstein. My mug was enough to make a child cry. Dating would truly be more challenging in my future.

It was time to get past the cosmetics. A large neurosurgeon with sandy-colored hair and a stoic bedside manner approached me. "We won't be operating on you. With all of your breaks, we would not even know where to start. Your spinal column is intact and not being impinged upon. We will place you in ICU and monitor your X-rays. We will hope there are no radical changes or shifts in your column. Now it is time for you to go on a morphine drip …"

"One question please. What is my long-term prognosis?"

"We don't know. We don't see many patients like you."

"Why is that?"

"Because they are usually dead."

I whispered a lame, "Oh!"

The next few days on the morphine drip were a haze of dreaming and snippets of reality thrown in. Concerned friends and family members phoned me. I have no recollection of the conversations. I do recall the nursing staff getting me up and out of bed. I even walked up a flight of steps under their watchful eyes. Best of all, my brother Mike arrived from New York City to take care of his "baby" brother. I wept shamelessly as he entered the room. He went on to prove once again why he is the best brother in the world.

Four days after the impact, I was discharged from the hospital. My post-discharge orders were written out and terse: "Do Not Remove the Brace!" It looked like sponge baths and partial shampoos would be my method of hygiene for awhile. Gross.

Mike and I began a 1,000-mile journey south to my old hometown of Fort Collins, Colo. He drove and I navigated. The plan was for me to get a second opinion from neurosurgeon number two and to convalesce in familiar surroundings.

I told Mike a few times: "I always wanted to take a road trip with you, but this is not what I had in mind."

Eight days after the accident, Mike and I listened to neurosurgeon number two, a no-nonsense, no-sugar-coating doctor who calls it like he sees it. He does not believe in small talk. I suppose after 35 years in the game, he has that right.

"Your vertebrae fractures are mild. You do have a definite broken sternum. I believe you will heal OK. We will take another set of X-rays in a few weeks to see if there are any changes. I doubt there will be. I'll see you again in three weeks."

In my former life, I worked for 28 years as a firefighter/EMT for the city of Fort Collins. In emergency services, the term "mechanism of injury" is bandied about to predict the outcome of an accident.

A small, 138-pound man being struck from behind by a sedan traveling at more than 50 mph is an obvious assault upon the body. Humans are not wired to survive such an ordeal. During my career, I went on calls for three similar bicycle accidents. For those unfortunate victims, there was no tomorrow. The one and only thing that separated me from them was my use of a bicycle helmet.

Now in Fort Collins, I meet former lovers, friends and acquaintances on the street. I smile grandly as I go to hug them. If the hug lingers long enough, I usually score a life affirming squeeze at the end. I make sure to pay back that squeeze in kind.

Second chances in life are precious. I do not wish to squander this one.

About the Author

Jeff Sambur's few worldly possessions live in Tucson, Ariz., throughout the year. Jeff pays them a visit for a few months each winter. The rest of the time he is on the road in Barley, a customized Ford van. Barley is fitted out with three backpacks, two bicycles, one laptop, heaps of maps, a comfy bed, fig bars, books, bananas, and, of course, cold beer.

Jeff can be reached for questions, comments and funny stories at jeffsambur@gmail.com. This is Jeff's first book.

12495586R00189

Made in the USA
Lexington, KY
16 December 2011